Welcome to Boston, Mr. Superintendent

WELCOME TO BOSTON, MR. SUPERINTENDENT

BY

JULIUS J. D'AGOSTINO

An account and study of an urban school system's turn-around in the first year of Robert S. Spillane's tenure as the Superintendent of Schools for the Boston public schools.

Welcome to Boston, Mr. Superintendent
An account and study of an urban school system's turnaround in the first year of Robert S. Spillane's tenure as the Superintendent of Schools for the Boston public schools.

The original draft of this book was a doctoral thesis accepted by Harvard University in 1983.

This is a work of non-fiction. It is based on real events and is drawn from a variety of sources including published materials and news reports, interviews and public documents. The views and opinions expressed are those of the individuals only and do not reflect or represent the views and opinions of a general or specific class.

Cover design by Elizabeth Glover

Special thanks to Jessica Culligan

Typeset by Swordsmith Productions
www.swordsmith.com

ISBN 978-1-4794-5287-3

First edition: October 2020

10 9 8 7 6 5 4 3 2 1

For Cathy

Table of Contents

Welcome to Boston, Mr. Superintendent

The Story

Introduction

When Robert R. "Bud" Spillane came to work on August 3, 1981, his first day as the new Boston Superintendent of Schools, he received a warm welcome. Stepping off of the elevator onto the fifth floor of school department headquarters at 26 Court Street, it was stiflingly apparent that the temperature was somewhere 90 degrees. Always the skeptic, he turned to the Chairperson of his Transition Team, and said, "Yeah, it figures. It's got to be sabotage."

Even though the air conditioner was repaired the next day, things got only hotter. By the end of the week, he had met with two school committee members, twice with the school attorney, his deputy superintendents, the school district business manager and breakfasted with the Mayor. He would need to recommend, at his first school committee meeting, the layoff of 1,070 teachers before the school year began in September. On top of that, school spending, regardless of the tempting rumors that floated back and forth from the Mayor's offices at Government Center and Court Street, would remain at the previous year's level of $210 million. Finally, the threat of a teachers' strike should not be taken lightly; there was a real possibility that more than five thousand teachers would strike in response to a layoff vote.

Behind each of these problems lay serious illnesses that gave Boston the reputation of being "one of the most troubled school systems in the nation" and a "national disgrace."[1] Spillane summarized it this way:

Why is Boston held in such low esteem?...Critics of our schools point to the weak leadership in many schools, a suffocating bureaucracy, a pitifully weak curriculum and staff development effort, and incoherent testing program, low expectations of students, poorly maintained buildings, and many other problems.... Perceptive observers of the Boston schools see a fundamental lack of accountability at all levels. They see a budget constantly in the red, with deficits routinely rolled over from year to year. They see students sliding from grade to grade without learning basic skills. They see teachers, some blatantly incompetent, not being held to account for their students' performance. They see principals unable or unwilling to take responsibility for the educational leadership of their schools. And they see administrators at all levels without the guts to move on poor performance.[2]

Boston: The City and its Actors

Boston has several identities.[3] It is one of the oldest cities in the nation yet claims cultural and artistic achievements and surrounds itself with some of the world's most prestigious universities.[4] It traces its roots back to the early pioneers of democratic governance but remains landlocked by tradition and a conservative ideology. "It takes a long time for things to happen here," a number of commentators revealed "change is slow; Boston is a small town."

Boston is a racially and ethnically mixed city. Its population of nearly 560,000 residents is 70 percent white, 22 percent black, and 8 percent non-black minorities. Boston's neighborhoods project this racial and ethnic mosaic and even underscore its socio-economic underpinnings. "They (neighborhoods) are Boston and its character," suggested one parent leader.

In the northern tier of Boston, white middle- and upper-income neighborhoods press against a heavy concentration of white low- and middle-income neighborhoods with sizeable ethnic enclaves like Irish-Americans and Italian-Americans. Especially in these ethnic neighborhoods, residents trace their heritage back a generation or two and proudly admit "this is where my parents grew up." The mosaic becomes more pronounced in the southern tier of the city. Black and white concentrations of low- and middle-income families are interspersed with Hispanic and Chinese populations. Small enclaves of low-income families dot the landscape where female-headed households sometimes comprise nearly

40 percent of all households. These neighborhoods press against other neighborhoods undergoing dramatic demographic changes that reveal a growing mixture of black and white middle- and upper middle-income families.

Only ten percent of the city's population sends its children to the public schools. Still, the school community, like the city itself, is divided by race and ethnicity. It is a factionalized school community, a collection of turfs. These turfs stand out like reflectors in the night, each a different color and intensity. Black and non-black minorities are represented by parent organizations like the influential Citywide Parents Advisory Council and the Hispanic El Comite. White and black parents (in the main, liberal-oriented) press their influence from organizations like the white-dominated Home-School Association and the Citywide Education Coalition and the black-dominated, community-based Freedom House.

Moreover, a 1974 Federal Court Desegregation Order, which relied on busing as a judicial remedy to desegregate the schools, heightened this diversity and prompted various neighborhood responses. More than 35,000 students left the school system in an eight-year period (1974–1982). The result of this decline left the schools with a 70 percent black and non-black minority population and a 30 percent white population. This stands in stark contrast to the city's population and creates two constituencies, each with different school expectations and leadership orientations.

One is the clients of the school system. In the main minorities, they seek program improvements based on educational equality and rely on the Federal court to promote their aims. A second constituency is the taxpayers. In the main, white, conservative-minded blue collar workers, they have pulled their children out of school (or have no children in school) and no longer want to see their tax dollars support a system that is predominantly black. This constituency represents a sizeable electorate and presses for budget reductions in order to control school spending and eliminate recurring deficits.

These constituencies focus school politics. The spring before Spillane arrived, a four-term Mayor threatened to close the schools when they ran out of money in April. He refused requests from the School Committee to increase the school budget for 1981–1982 beyond its present $210 million appropriation. Influential business organizations like the Trilateral Council for Quality Education and the Coordinating Committee supported the Mayor's initiatives. In response, the School Committee cut programs and closed 27 schools in the wake of declining enrollments.

Race and ethnicity characterized school appointments and promotions in the school system Spillane took over. One school commentator pointed to the school committee that was dominated by white conservative incumbents as an institution founded on patronage. Indeed, others noted, it was a system ravaged by personal prerogatives which took priority over educational and financial responsibility.

Spillane worked with two school committees. The first included two white (anti-busing) conservatives, John McDonough and Elvira "Pixie" Palladino; a black, John D. O'Bryant; and two white liberal members, Jean Sullivan McKeigue and Kevin McCluskey. (McCluskey was appointed in October, 1980, to complete the term of Gerald O'Leary, the original third conservative anti-busing coalition member, who lost his seat when he was convicted for bribery and extortion related to a vote for a new bus contract.) The School Committee generally reflected the more broadly conservative climate of the city and even McKeigue and McCluskey, votes suggested, reflected the financial mood of the city's taxpayers. The committee also reflected a changing emphasis toward patronage. With the loss of O'Leary and the subsequent indictment of McDonough for alleged participation in the bus scandal, the white conservative coalition lost their hold over the committee and the personal prerogatives it provided them.

The November, 1981, elections dramatically changed the orientation of the School Committee. McKeigue, O'Bryant and McCluskey were re-elected. They were joined by a conservative-minded and former Home-School Association President, Rita Walsh-Tomasini, and a second black, Jean McGuire. The new committee took office January 1, 1982, and emphasized a commitment toward educational priorities and financial responsibility.

The emergence of two blacks in positions of school leadership brought a new dimension to school politics; both O'Bryant and McGuire were education-oriented, progressive-minded and committed to minority interests. The election prompted one reporter to write,

> Boston [at last] finally may have a school committee majority...which appears to signal a change in [its] political environment from conservative to liberal...[5]

The election was an opportunity for the School Committee to exert a new type of leadership—a black-white progressive coalition. But the coalition never emerged because each member had different commitments, different constituencies. In short, new personal prerogatives surfaced to obviate the changing emphasis toward patronage.

Spillane was the fourth superintendent to take the helm of the Boston Public Schools in a 14-month period. Robert Wood, hired in June, 1978 for a four-year term, left in August, 1980. He left amid controversy and allegations for failing to bring the budget under control; however, school commentators revealed that Wood lost the support of John McDonough, president of the School Committee, because he (Wood) mistreated McDonough's brother, Joseph McDonough, an acting deputy superintendent.

Paul Kennedy, a long-time and well-respected administrator in the Boston Public Schools, took over in August, 1980. Still in the throes of reorganizing his office with administrators close to him (and McDonough), he died suddenly in March, 1981. Joseph McDonough followed Kennedy as Acting Superintendent of Schools until June, 1981. McDonough made some inroads into the financial problems facing the Boston schools, but he could not quell the tide of discontent expressed by the Mayor and other constituencies. Spillane's contract began on August 1, 1981 to complete the eleven months remaining on Wood's term. (Boston city ordinances required that he complete the unexpired term before he could be eligible for a four-year contract.) On his desk was the same issue that his predecessor faced.

Chapter 1
Teacher Layoffs

Spillane's first public appearance as superintendent of schools came five days after he took the job. The headlines read: "Welcome to Boston, Mr. Superintendent"; the article scored,

> *Newly-named school superintendent, Robert Spillane, got his first exposure to Boston-style controversy yesterday at a tumultuous hearing on a plan to dismiss more than 1,000 teachers. Spillane, who received a cordial reception from the 600 [black armband wearing] teachers...heard School Committee President, John O'Bryant insist that the layoffs were the only way to keep the school department from plunging deep into a fiscal hole from the very start of the school year.[1]*

Even though the layoffs were recommended (to the School Committee) before he arrived, Spillane pushed for their approval. For the next two weeks (prior to a formal vote of the School Committee), the layoff issue was hotly debated in the media.

The Boston Teachers Union (BTU) challenged the layoffs saying they breached the contract signed with the School Committee. The contract included a "job security clause" that protected tenured teachers from layoffs until June, 1982. In addition, they accused Mayor White of "putting the system through torture"[2] since he refused to act on school committee requests for supplemental funds that could defer the layoffs.

At a second hearing, attended by more than 1,500 teachers, tempers flared. "Instead of looking at your budget and taking a calm, sane approach," shouted Kathleen Kelley, BTU President, "you decided to use a meat cleaver."[3] Kelley's reference to "looking at your budget" was predicted on the BTU's claim that money to defer the layoffs was available.

She said their investigation of the budget revealed nearly $10 million was overestimated for non-salary items. Still despair reigned as teachers threatened to "devote every waking moment…to make sure that anyone of you who votes to have us laid off will be permanently fired" (all school committee members came up for re-election later in November).[4]

Uncertainty surrounded the two weeks prior to the vote of the School Committee. Two judicial rulings, which influenced the layoff proceedings, were being appealed by the BTU. One was the Suffolk County Superior Court ruling that the BTU's "job security clause" was unenforceable because it conflicted with management prerogatives at the time the school department had insufficient funds. Another, Judge Garrity, the Federal court judge supervising the desegregation order, ruled that any layoff must respect the School Department's ratio of 20 percent black to 80 percent white teachers. This meant that the "seniority clause" had to give way to affirmative action guidelines established by the court. Consequently, white teachers with more years of experience were slated for layoff while black teachers with much less experience would keep their jobs. The BTU, outraged by the decision, announced: "This union will take a position of strict seniority…white teachers with years of seniority are going to lose their jobs over an injustice (segregation) not perpetrated by them."[5]

The Superior Court ruled the layoffs had to conform to State law: each School Committee member had to attend the hearings to be eligible to vote and a two-thirds majority was required to carry the vote. With one member absent from the hearings, Spillane needed a unanimous (4–0) vote to carry the layoffs.

One School Committee member, Pixie Palladino, it was rumored, would vote "no." An anti-busing activist, she made it clear she was opposed to the layoffs because they violated seniority provisions of the contract in favor of affirmative action. The rest of the School Committee, except for its president, John O'Bryant, was non-committal. The challenge facing Spillane was simple, commented one reporter:

> If he strikes out, if the teachers come back, then the Boston school system cannot possibly stay within its agreed upon $210 million budget…[6]

The School Committee met on August 18, 1981, amid jeering and shouts from more than 500 angry teachers. One reporter noted,

> *A hush came over the 500 angry, noisy teachers yesterday after Spillane, Committee President John D. O'Bryant, and Committeeman Kevin H. McCluskey had spoken in favor of the layoffs. Now it was Palladino's turn…[speaking in favor] Her remarks were met with a howl of boos and catcalls. Palladino shouted back, demanding that the hecklers "shut up" to let her get in another word.[7]*

The School Committee voted 4–0 to layoff 710 permanent (tenured) teachers and 360 provisional teachers. It was an uneasy victory for the School Committee and Spillane. "Almost every member of the School Committee has been threatened…it's a very scary thing," commented O'Bryant.[8] Spillane, commenting on the hesitancy of the School Committee to express favor with the layoffs, said that "it (uncertainty) is certainly a form of torture…politics has a very definite role in school decisions."[9] But the hesitancy was a ploy by the School Committee. The School Committee would have liked to avoid the layoffs and maintain leverage at the polls. Their silence was a way to force Spillane to retreat from his position of recommending the layoffs, for him to say: "why should I stick my neck out." The hesitancy forced him to choose to "take his case to the public,"[10] as one reporter recommended, or confront the School Committee. He confronted the School Committee.

> *I had to get four out of four votes…so I had to get the School Committee together, just us in a room, just the five of us, not the staff…and I reminded them how important it was from their perspective and from mine…and, I threatened them. I reminded them of the crisis they had last April when they didn't have enough money to run the schools and the Mayor threatened to close the schools…*

The layoffs were both an economic and political issue. As an economic issue, the layoffs represented a substantial reduction in the school budget so that Spillane could live within his allocation. "The BTU," commented one school official, "just didn't take that $210 million budget crisis seriously." The layoffs could be justified in terms of current enrollment statistics; while the school population declined by 14,000 students in the six-year period that preceded Spillane (1975–1981), the teaching staff increased by 100. As a result, the layoffs meant that the school department had to "adjust all at once, along with a forced move by Mayor White to limit spending." Spillane noted, "the layoffs were just that we had too many people...even after the layoffs, the class size was 25:1, which isn't too bad for this system."

The layoffs were politically important to Spillane. It sent a signal to the Mayor and the public that he would live within a $210 million budget. It was also a signal to the school department. "He knew what he had to do," recalls one official. "He was saying that what we have to do is make the system accountable; we must learn to live within our budget." They meant Spillane could avoid the school closing crisis of the previous year. He needed to avoid a similar crisis (which happened under a $210 million budget) if he was to build his credibility and win a four-year contract. They also gave Spillane a way to redirect program initiatives. The programs being dismantled through the layoffs (specialized programs in art, music and others) could re-emerge according to his own plans for curriculum redesign. Finally, though unexpectedly, the layoffs forced a strategy to exercise his administrative authority with the School Committee.

> They never tell each other anything, how they're going to vote. There's a lot of history to that...a general distrust. I was trying to get them to look at working together as a unified group. For the most part, they were five different corporations and the superintendent had to negotiate with five corporations. This [layoffs] forced them to come together.

A week after the vote, on August 26, 1981, in an upbeat speech to the administrative staff, Spillane outlined his priorities for the school year. Noting that the layoffs were a "tragic loss" for the school system, he pressed that the school system will go forward with a new focus.[11] But the BTU, still recoiling from a nearly 20 percent reduction-in-force, was planning other things. The day after the speech, the BTU Executive Board announced it was calling a meeting at which time the Board would recommend a strike. The meeting was set for September 7, two days before school was to open.

Spillane was in his office with two aides when he got the news. One official remembered,

> *Bud was standing over at the corner of his office and I went up to them and told them I just got the news that the union executive board voted to recommend a strike. Bud stood there; after a moment he went in and dialed Betcher (school attorney) and asked him two questions. When he got off the phone, he turned to us and said to just give him ten minutes and with that he closed the door and left us standing there. When he came out, he ushered us in with some press people who had just arrived...got us into his office and said, "If they strike, then I'll fire them with no amnesty."*

The threat of a strike surrounded the layoffs even though an official declaration was not made until after the layoff vote. The Chairperson of the Transition Team, commented, that

> *even the first week on the job, the threat of a teachers' strike dominated our attention...it was brewing even though it didn't hit the newspapers until late in August...we (Transition Team) advised him not to take the risk (and try to avoid the layoffs)...he was a new superintendent and to start with a strike was bad...*

The *Boston Herald American* heralded Spillane's response with the headlines: "Spillane's Warning: Teach or Be Fired."[12] It reported that if a strike were to come, Spillane would open the schools anyway. "There are plenty of good teachers out there who want to work," it quoted Spillane as saying. "If the teachers who are supposed to be in the classrooms are not there, I will bring in new teachers."[13]

The threat of a strike, while not welcomed by Spillane, was an opportunity to confront the BTU on the important issues of job security and seniority. Spillane felt that these were intrusions on his authority to manage the schools system. He stressed that the job security clause was overly restrictive on a school system faced with financial woes. He argued, "It is clear that in the teacher's contract under the job security clause that if there was no funding available, job security does not exist..."[14] He then added, "As far as I'm concerned, a strike would be illegal and would be met with a firm position from me."[15] The BTU stood firm. Kelley predicted, "If a strike is approved by the union's membership, it will last as long as it takes for us to get justice…Our contract has been violated."[16]

The seniority issue was equally troublesome for Spillane. In order to breach the seniority provision, he had to face a collision he felt he could not avoid. Dentler and Scott, with unusual prescience, noted two years earlier,

> *Because of the court order, black teachers, although mostly recent hires, will not be the first fired. It will be a major test of BTU reasonableness, however, to remain silent while white tenured teachers are terminated and newcoming blacks are retained.*[17]

The strike, then, was "the crossroads where two revolutions—unionism and desegregative racial justice—met and collided."[18] The Concerned Black Educators of Boston (CBEB) as well as the Black Educators Alliance of Massachusetts (BEAM) announced they would not support the strike. Joseph Delgardo, president of BEAM, noted that his organization's position is not anti-union, just opposed to the strike. It would be "counterproductive," "ineffective" and "directed in part at the faculty desegregation order of the Federal Court."[19] As a result, racial tension surrounded Spillane's attempt to break the back of the seniority provision, a critical issue for the BTU.

Voices were raised during the week that preceded the strike vote. Kelley proposed additional meetings with Spillane, but he responded, "There's nothing left to discuss…the law is clear and I'm confident common sense will prevail."[20] The *Boston Herald American* published its survey on the strike vote: "Of the 585 responses, 404 said striking teachers should be dismissed. Only 145 felt…money should be found in the budget to pay their salaries."[21] The Boston newspapers urged Mayor White to intercede; he did not. In addition, they urged teachers to avoid the strike. Parent advocacy groups supported Spillane, and many observers thought that President Reagan's strong position against striking Federal Air Controllers the previous summer influenced Spillane. One school observer commented that "he (Spillane) is a public administrator who senses public support for the hard line…"[22]

Barely five weeks on the job, Spillane thrust the school system into a tailspin. It is a risk. Even though white teachers outnumbered black teachers four to one, the possibility of a white teacher manning picket lines while black teachers entered schools (and crossed the picket lines) made some school officials hesitate to support Spillane. The Transition Team Chairperson analyzed the situation this way:

It was an interesting choice. It (strike) could devastate him or the union. It was a question of a real social confrontation in that blacks would not go in sympathy with the teachers…it could affect the whole system…it was risky.

The strike vote also became a leadership question for Kelley. One BTU official claimed "If they (Executive Board) don't get a strike vote, it's a vote of no confidence in her."[23] "In fact, Kelley didn't want the strike," commented one university official. "She was looking for a way to get out…she had to save face and go back to the troops with something…but what did he do, he called her bluff. I'm not sure that was in the best interests of the district."

The BTU voted on September 7 not to strike. However, in a series of confusing votes, the membership set September 21 for a system-wide walkout and authorized the BTU Executive Board to continue discussions with Spillane. If the discussions prove successful, the Executive Board could call off the walkout but would have to convene the membership to explain why. If the discussions were not successful, the walkout stood without another meeting.

It was a clever political maneuver that kept the pressure on Spillane. Likewise, it also meant more waiting and worrying for parents. To parents, the strike threat (and delay) was a continuation of the problems of the previous year when Mayor White refused to increase the 1981–82 budget (Spillane's first year). As a result, the spring before Spillane arrived, the School Committee cut programs and closed schools in the wake of declining enrollments.

Schools opened on September 9 amid this background. It was a chaotic beginning that threatened to undo Spillane's position against the BTU. The layoffs compounded an already poor personnel record system so that teacher assignments were inaccurate and confusing. The week before the September 7 strike vote, Spillane realized that many schools would be plagued by misassignments. School administrators found that teachers were misplaced and, in some cases, classrooms were without any teachers at all.

Unmanned classrooms, unassigned teachers and a general staffing confusion surrounded the opening of school. This raised the ire of parent advocacy groups who were supporting Spillane's position against the strike. In one case, parents threatened to sit in at Spillane's office until he could tell them why their school lacked teachers. To add to the confusion, parents were forced to become bus monitors and crossing guards because program cuts included a reduction of these school personnel. Administrators were plagued by an upsurge of fights due to a cutback in security personnel. One parent put it this way: "How can kids learn with all these disruptions?"[24]

The chaotic opening of school was attributed to the layoffs but there were other reasons. Classrooms were reported to enroll as many as fifty to sixty students. One school official commented, "The court order severely restricted us and our ability to move kids around so we couldn't adjust assignments (on the basis of the layoffs)...We had teachers servicing a handful of kids and a few overcrowded classrooms caused by the geocodes (student assignments based on racial quotas). Parents fell in support of the BTU who claimed that class sizes were in excess of contract provisions.

The BTU contract was another reason for the chaotic opening of school. The contract gives teachers "attachment rights" and "assignment rights." Attachments rights protected teachers against transfer if their seniority was greater than someone else who wanted to replace them. Assignment rights allowed teachers to pick schools on the basis of their seniority. The assignment rights were especially troublesome. Spillane noted,

The pool (assignment pool) situation—assignment of teachers to various schools is done on the basis of the teacher selecting the schools rather than the principal selecting the teacher. Teachers should have options to

note what schools they prefer but the principal or administrator should have rejection rights.[25]

"What happened then," commented one school official, "was a second grade teacher, who had taught second grade all her life but had seniority, would end up teaching high school English because there were no second grade classes and she had certification in English."

The opening of school intensified the efforts of both the BTU and the School Committee to wrangle more money out of the Mayor. It was not to be; the Mayor just could not "bail out" the schools while he was laying off police and firefighters in the wake of the state-mandated tax cutting law (Proposition 2 ½).

Spillane used the two weeks to shore up the strength he needed to avoid the strike. He fulfilled his promises to restore (with School Committee approval) 125 jobs that had been cut from the budget. The move designed to soften the impact of the teacher layoffs was possible because $3 million was overestimated for non-salary items in the 1981–82 budget. But, he also re-affirmed his position that striking teachers would be fired and added that the school department would not provide striking teachers with severance pay. Kelley noted,

My sense, intellectually, is that with dropping enrollments and (fiscal) problems in the city, that we were living on borrowed time…but the final straw that developed a lot of bitterness and anger…even beyond just losing a career was his view of not giving severance and not easing the transition of teachers out of the system…that sent the worst chill through the system…it put us on guard and projected a different view of Spillane.

Spillane and the BTU Executive Board met regularly during the two weeks. Spillane felt confident and noted "the BTU can show much progress in the last two weeks. We're closer to understanding what's in the budget."[26] Kelley was less optimistic. Three days before the scheduled vote, she, along with 250 teachers and sympathizers, surrounded school department headquarters pressing the issue of layoffs and seniority.

The teachers voted 1404 to 836 to reject a strike call by the union leadership. The vote divided the staff. Many laid off teachers expressed bitterness toward their colleagues who had jobs and did not support the strike. The vote caused intense resentment toward many less-experienced black teachers who did not support the strike and heightened an already tense racial issue surrounding the controversy.

Spillane saw the layoff and the threat of a strike as a way to confront the BTU over management rights. One observer felt Spillane knew he was headed for collision with the BTU and pictured him

> *looking into a crystal ball, looking at the future when he first came. He asks himself "What do I have to do; well, I see the contract is the problem. There's no management control here. The God damn School Committee gave it all away. I've got to be tough; I've got to use the first year to get at it and prepare for later years. My first year, I've got to start doing it…can't wait for negotiations next year. I must look tough now." Boy, I mean when he said those teachers better be there or they'll be fired, they believed him.*

One parent advocacy leader recalled that when she sat in on screening committees to hire central office staff like attorneys and collective bargaining personnel, the key questions were: Did you ever have to stop a union from coming in? How did you do it? Did you ever have to get a union to give up rights? How did you do it?

In an interview later in the year, he recalled,

> *I've been called a union-buster. And, if union-busting means I want to eliminate the seniority clause…then I'll take the rap. But, that isn't union busting. That's just having a sensible contract (for dismissal and promotion) that makes the management of the system more effective…*[27]

While the threat of a strike disappeared, the layoffs did not. On three more occasions, Spillane recommended layoffs. In October and February, Spillane recommended the layoff of 94 and 84 teachers, respectively. These layoff recommendations were the result of inaccuracies in the September layoff request. He noted, "We made the mistake because we were so fouled up…when I first came in here we laid off the wrong people. We laid off people who were more senior and kept others on."

On both occasions, however, the School Committee rejected his layoff recommendations. Spillane's failure to provide an accurate spending rate which could expose the possibility of a year-end deficit and a need for the layoffs plus low teacher morale were important criteria for the School Committee. He noted,

I'm not sure they didn't think I was moving a bit too quickly—a bit too harshly and I recognized that so I took the loss…But it was important politically and publicly to make certain that everyone knew that that's really what we had to do and I was prepared to recommend it.

The third layoff vote came in June of Spillane's first year when he recommended and the School Committee approved the dismissal of 795 teachers. He recollected about these votes and noted they were difficult for the School Committee. "There just had never been a layoff," he said. "They just weren't used to it and it was just very difficult…But the difference was when it came to the end of the year and I got a unanimous vote on 750 layoffs."

There were obvious tradeoffs. The layoff strategy eventually earned him the disdain of the BTU. It became a rallying point for the protection of the seniority clause. The BTU never wavered in their position of seniority, and it kept Spillane off balance. They redefined a management issue at the local level into a broad national labor issue; as a result, they drew support from other unions in the district and in other cities (i.e., New York City).

The strategy also forced the BTU to seek new allies and promote a coalition with parent advocacy groups and the Boston City Council. Even though they lost their struggle to prevent the layoff of 795 teachers in June, their appearance was much different. Throughout the weeks prior to the layoff vote, the BTU, along with parent advocacy groups, criticized Spillane for victimizing students, parents and teachers and accused him of being "uncaring and unprofessional."[28] At a hearing held by the Boston City Council, Spillane was chastised for "not being much more than a puppet for the Mayor," while one city councilor advised him "that it's time to stand up to the Mayor." [29] Meanwhile, the BTU lobbied the Boston City Council over a plan Spillane (and the Mayor) proposed that considered 1982–83 budget increases as a one-time expense rather than added to the base ($210 million) budget. If approved, the BTU would have had a more narrow base from which to negotiate. The BTU, in an unusual alliance, got the support of the city council and convinced them to reject the plan, which they did. But budget issues still remained unsolved.

Chapter 2
A Nightmare

A team of 23 consultants hired by Boston's new school superintendent for a three-day project this fall were denied rooms at the Midtown Motor Inn because the school department had a poor credit record... Embarrassed and angered when the motel refused to register the consultants, Spillane convinced the manager that a check for $3,800 would be at the hotel office first thing the next morning.[1]

Although a few hours late, the Midtown Motor Inn did get its check for $3,800. It took Spillane a day to track down the bottleneck. What he learned was that creditors were demanding payment in advance because the school department had developed a reputation for not paying its bills.

Who's in Charge?

Deficit spending in Boston, both at the municipal level as well as the school department, is a financial tradition. City documents refer to this annual practice as a "prior year appropriation deficit" as to say it is just a matter of not getting enough in the first place. However, where the city would habitually overspend by 1–2 percent, the school department took greater liberties. In 1980–1981, the year prior to Spillane's arrival, the school department overspend its budget by 12.3 percent.

To many observers, the lack of control over school spending was not a mystery. A report, published by the Boston Municipal Research Bureau (BMRB), which greeted Spillane when he took office, pointed out that the schools were unable to control the number of people on the payroll; too many key management positions in the school system still are filled with persons who lack training for, and experience in, the jobs they hold; and, financial control procedures...are lacking in the school system.[2]

The report went on to say that "In the budget year that ended June 30 (1981), the school system exceeded its $210 million appropriation by an estimated $20 million."[3]

Spillane did not welcome this news nor did he welcome the discoveries he made soon after he arrived. *The Boston Globe* reported on August 15, 1981,

> *Spillane, about two weeks on the job, acknowledges that while he had heard all the horror stories about the state of affairs in the school department, he is nonetheless surprised. "I expected that there would be at least manual records and some correlation between personnel, payroll and budget. The records aren't there."[4]*

He told me what he meant by "The records aren't there" and, more importantly, why they were not there.

> *Someone left last March and was getting paid when I came here. That's a reflection on personnel and somewhat of a throw-back to the patronage system...The Personnel [office] may have known all 5,000 staff and did little favors without reflecting on the budget...for example, a person is hired but no determination is made if the budget could afford it...elsewhere you could go to jail for overspending your budget.*

School officials, prior to his arrival, confessed, "It is still possible for various offices of the school department to have new personnel put on payroll without the budget office approving the hiring"; little favors were kept private. One former Boston School Superintendent tells why in an article he wrote about his experiences.

> *The [school] committee functions as a small sub-system of local politics, with a built-in constituency important at the margin, in-ward looking, highly dependent on home recognition...In exchange for campaign support was internal support for career advancement...If a [school employee] has clearly demonstrated motivation only at the highest public interest—as many do—a historical venerable pattern of appeals "upstairs" to*

the eleventh floor (school committee offices at 26 Court Street) of the most mundane of personnel decisions continues.[5]

Spillane reflected on this practice of patronage.

Well, you still see patronage. All you have to do is look around. [But] all patronage isn't bad...Patronage is taking care of your own in the sense of Boston residents...Someone you know can do a job and why shouldn't they get the job. But patronage, historically, in Boston, had been abused. It didn't have any qualifications attached to it. It was, you're my friend, you're my supporter, you're my ally...or whatever and therefore I'll get you a job...There wasn't really any qualification.

Many of the practices Spillane inherited were left over from an organizational scheme that encouraged this lack of control over school spending. Prior to changes made in 1978, the Boston City Charter did not give the school superintendent responsibility over personnel, business management (budget) and plant operations.[6] These functions operated independently of the superintendent; each had its own staff and reported directly to the school committee. In addition, all civil service employees, commonly a patronage warehouse, were hired directly by the school committee. The superintendent was not allowed to remove (dismiss) any employee without school committee approval. Assured by the city charter of an annual budget equal to that of the preceding year, the school committee had great latitude to spend freely in order to court loyalty. One observer close to the school system put it this way:

It was a terrible system. Each office had its own administrative assistant...The Business Manager used to carry a budget in his shirt pocket and when certain school committee members wanted someone hired, under the old patronage system, he would hire them. So they didn't have any idea of who they had on staff or how much they were spending...they designed the system that way.

In 1978, the Massachusetts legislature passed Chapter 333 of the Acts and Resolves of the Commonwealth. For the first time in Boston's history, the superintendent was elected to a stated four-year term; he or she could dismiss (but not appoint) key senior officials at will, and, for the first time, the superintendent had responsibilities over the business operations of the department as well as academic operations.[7]

But the incumbents in the tripartite administrative structure remained. Spillane noted, "There were three different systems on the computer: one for budget, one for the business manager and one for the personnel director and it wasn't all tied together...They were independent with their own turfs." At least two school superintendents before Spillane tried to pull together the three functions—budget, payroll and personnel—but little impact was made. One school official guessed that "it was to their advantage to keep that level of chaos."

In Boston, the lack of control over these areas was the reason for the debilitating financial chaos that existed. It took its toll on a number of individuals and groups. To the business community, severe overspending by the school department was a threat to the financial credibility of the city. One businessman commented, "you've got to realize that bonding agencies [in this city] study the fiscal situation. They are uncertain that the city can meet its obligations with recent school committee practices...they just have to solve the problem."

Mayor White also sent signals to Spillane "to put his financial house in order." Faced with a legislative mandate, called Massachusetts Proposition 2 ½, designed to cut taxes, municipal departments were undergoing serious retrenchment. The Mayor could no longer afford to reconcile school deficits "by subterranean transfers among accounts well after the close of the fiscal year" while he was reducing police and fire services.[8] He refused to fund a new school budget (1981–1982, Spillane's first year) beyond its present appropriation of $210 million. In doing so, he was criticized by teachers and parents for imposing an "arbitrary" ceiling on the budget.

Even the school committee suffered at the hands of a "runaway budget." The previous spring, the Mayor threatened to close the schools when they "ran out of money" in April. This impaired their image at a time when they were beginning to focus on financial control and responsibility.

The budget control mess brought out the "hidden years" of woeful spending practices by former school committees. Even though the present school committee signaled a changing philosophy, Mayor White still pushed for some dramatic changes. Under the Tregor Bill, a home-rule petition (legislation particular to the city of Boston) proposed early in Spillane's term in order to alleviate a $50 million tax abatement problem the city faced, the Mayor added an important caveat: the power to hire and fire Boston school department employees would be transferred from the school committee to the superintendent. It was a significant effort and a school official said privately "that the change is the most dramatic reform of the school committee in a century. It means the end of school committee patronage. People have been trying to get at that for years."[9]

But the Tregor Bill went through more than a half-dozen changes, and by the end of Spillane's first year, Tregor was approved without an increase in Spillane's power. Spillane, who took a neutral stance on the issue against the advice of the Mayor and the business community, was perceptive in his assessment.

> *It would have been wrong for me to jump on it; but also, politically, if I had come out for it and you were a resident or a politician you'd say, "Hey wait a minute, this guy just came from New York, he wants to take over the schools. We just elected five school committee members and it doesn't mean anything, my vote doesn't mean anything in the management of this business…"*

The budget control process is a technical process that requires the mind-set of a comptroller. But it is also a political process. Budget and personnel are in Boston, as they are in many urban school systems, bases of power. These functions have control over vital services and leverage over how policy is implemented. Budget and personnel also have the requisite ability to hide important information as much as they have the ability to reveal information. It seems clear from what Spillane did that he recognized budget control as a political process.

He got the support of the school committee that hired him to "straighten out the mess" even though two members could trace their tenure back to pre-1978 days. When these two members were defeated mid-way through Spillane's first year, he became even "more golden." In contrast to previous school committees, this school committee wanted to march to the beat of a different drummer—fiscal responsibility.

He got the business community to volunteer staff to improve the financial management program. In a first for Boston, the business community and the Boston school department instituted an Executive-on-Loan-program. This program brought to the school department key financial managers to help develop new systems and improve existing budget control systems.

Spillane also made some important staff changes. He directed the management information services chief to plan and implement a new automated system of budget control. He replaced middle management staff with limited training and experience in fiscal operations with accountants and computer programmers. He promoted some employees, kept others and reorganized the budget and personnel functions so they reported to a Deputy Superintendent for Finance Administration. In doing so, he consolidated his authority over the financial operations of the school system.

He replaced the personnel manager with someone who brought professional personnel management skills to his office. The personnel position, in particular, was important. More than 75 percent of the budget was tied to personnel costs and any effort to bring spending under control meant controlling personnel information. "There was a real void there in information," commented one school official. "No one previously knew how many people were on the payroll or in some cases who they were…what their experience and certification was, or how much money we were spending [in this area]."

Finally Spillane built some bridges that were important to him. He found the payroll was always late: "They used to send it over there and it was put on the bottom of the pile, if it ever got on the pile. So when I came here I called the city auditor and we went out for breakfast. I established a relationship with him. Since then the payroll has not been late…oh yes, sometimes, but he calls me and says, look Bud, I got this problem. So we get it in the p.m. and not the a.m.; or I'll say don't push it."

These moves helped Spillane change the balance of power; he weakened the tripartite administrative structure of personnel-budget-payroll that he inherited and moved budgetary decision making closer to his office. In doing so, he began to neutralize the effects of patronage. To be sure, the school committee's desire to correct the budget spending problem gave him a leg-up on this effort. He used this weakness and school committee support to dismiss and reassign staff who benefited from patronage.

Spillane also pushed for a series of changes in the technical operations budget including upgrading the staffing system to support a computerized system; updating personnel records; and establishing a system of prior approval before jobs were filled.

Spillane used these moves to bring spending under control. Some people I spoke to said this was important to do as soon as he took over the job: "Financial credibility was the most important issue, maybe the biggest issue. He couldn't get to the other issues unless he had some believers."

By December, still in the throes of making changes and initiating controls, he predicted a $2.3 million deficit for his first year. "The news from the School Department," said *The Boston Globe*, "was not merely good; in context, it was exceptional."[10] For Spillane, it meant he could now take aim at getting credibility with the Mayor.

I'll Live With It!

Throughout the fall, Spillane confessed that he could not assess accurately the spending rate of the school department. This troubled him deeply since he was adamant about requiring the school department "to know where it stood and how much it was going to spend." It also played an important role in how he approached the Mayor.

The Boston school department's budget is limited by legislation which says that the Mayor must fund an annual appropriation equal to the spending level of the previous year. Supplemental funds needed during the course of the year must be approved by the Mayor and city council.

It is these supplemental budgets that focus the budget each year. It was clear to Spillane from the previous year (overspent by $26 million) that "the $210 million ceiling on school spending imposed by Mayor White [was] simply not sufficient to run [the Boston Schools]."[11] But Spillane refused to ask for additional funds. He commented after two weeks on the job: "I told the Mayor that I will not talk money with him until I had a better idea of what a $210 million budget looked like and what our spending rate was."[12]

Instead, he went about preparing for the worst. He pushed for reductions in anticipation that spending would exceed the budget. He pushed the school committee to honor their pledge to layoff 1,070 teachers in an effort to control spending. He made sizeable program cuts in athletics and physical education, elementary reading, vocational-occupational education, security forces and traffic aides and eliminated the kindergarten program. He was criticized by the press and by many groups, but the loudest objections came from parents who vociferously extolled the virtues of these programs at the meetings he held with them in each district.

Spillane made living under a $210 million budget a top priority. It was important to signal to both the school department and the school committee that, given its history, the school department was serious about living under its budget. It was also important to build credibility with certain groups. Spillane's commitment to a $210 million budget earned him credibility with the Mayor and business community. They saw this commitment as a way to impose financial responsibility on the school system.

This strategy also meant Spillane had to make tradeoffs. The layoffs, which were critical for staying within the budget, meant gaining leverage with the Mayor and others at the expense of building teacher morale. Spillane agreed to this assessment. He noted, "The morale problem couldn't be avoided. Some things can be avoided, some things cannot. One must decide and act rather than try to wait it out so some magical solution comes."

He made another tradeoff. By opting for severe program cuts, he raised the ire of parents and community organizations throughout the city. However, this action won him support from those parents who did not have children in school. This constituency represented 90 percent of the city's population and gave him significant taxpayer support. He felt this support was important:

> *In reality only 10% of the city has kids in school so that means most don't have them in school. You've got to get them to say "OK, that sounds good…I'll support you."*

Spillane knew that the budget process was a political process. One observer commented that it is important "to relate the budget to the political activity that goes on in Boston. You always heard that the superintendent needs more money and the Mayor saying there was a lot of fat and waste…so he had to work with them." Spillane was more specific: "The Mayor is critical. The Mayor controls education because he has the dollars. He can starve the system; he can make it undernourished by not giving it all it needs…"

Spillane was exchanging long-term gains for short-term losses. "I guess in a way, it was a rational approach to administration…he made the hard choices," commented one businessman. In exchange for support from the Mayor and the business community, Spillane was willing to concede to program and staff reductions. He stood as a "lightning rod for the schools and took some of the heat off the Mayor for not funding the schools." Likewise, the business community benefitted; with spending under control, they felt more willing to become partners with the school and later in Spillane's first year committed more than $300,000 for a Teacher Award program. In this way they could turn around their own poor image. One city council member put it this way:

> *The business community had not given special attention to the schools and they were beginning to get some heat about that…people were complaining that most of them lived outside the city of Boston [but made their living in Boston]…they gave a cold shoulder to public education in this city…"*

Spillane stayed within the $210 million budget he got to run the schools in the first year. He did not "take on the Mayor" as some wanted him to do in order to get a supplemental budget. Nor did he fall victim to the cries of parent groups. In the end, he avoided the school closing crisis that plagued the school system the year before. "This was important," he told me, "avoiding the crisis and getting credibility so that we could get the $5 million (a 1982–93 supplemental allocation) and so that I could get the business community to give $300,000…this money is going to just pay off tremendously in the future."

Chapter 3
The Chess Board

...I don't believe in the honeymoon theory anyway. It's always fun to talk about that and to use it in speeches but if I did believe in a honeymoon theory I would say my honeymoon started six months after I was on the job...when I built some credibility...I think that the first six months you learn about the place. They knew it was a disaster; it was an all out war. But there wasn't any front. I mean we were getting shot at in all kinds of ways...[it] was just so bad that you had to just start working and put things together and doing it sometimes in lump sums, sometimes piece by piece...I just made certain that part of my job was to see that personnel was in shape.

Spillane relied heavily on his Transition Team. Organized in August, the Transition Team only existed for six weeks and produced a document of less than eighty pages. By comparison, one school official noted, "it was in stark contrast to the more than six inches of documents" that a previous superintendent used in the first year as the Boston School Superintendent. It was a document relatively devoid of the usual characteristic data: budget figures, personnel numbers, position descriptions, historical reference and short- and long-range planning suggestions. It was an "action document" that probed and peeked into the organization at all levels and found "the weakest points in the system...the obvious areas that everyone knew were weak, dysfunctioning and anti-productive." Spillane felt that there had to be "some general agreement about these weaknesses" and that by finding them he could find that "fifty percent of the organization that will look to torpedo you."

Transition Teams are usually brought on prior to a new superintendent beginning his or her tenure, at least ninety days before. Spillane's Transition Team started the day he started. But, an apparent disadvantage turned out to be a decided advantage to him. Working side by side with the Transition Team, Spillane spent countless hours with the Transition Team Chairperson. This allowed him to confirm or disprove his own diagnosis of the organization. He told me,

> I wanted to know what was happening…what had to be addressed…I used it as a management tool. I talked with [the chairperson] everyday…found out who he talked with, told him who to talk with, who to see, who would be very solid in the organization. I gave him my impressions and he told me what was wrong, how to correct it and how to change it…that was important. I was able to look into the organization with more than one pair of eyes and find out this one is weak and doesn't have any management skills…okay, that explains that…

Spillane used the Transition Team to his advantage. As a management tool, he could quickly assess operations as well as the individuals who "made it work and didn't make it work." Spillane relied on a Transition Team that included both outsiders and insiders. Outsiders provided an objective and fresh perspective while insiders offered an organizational perspective and identified historical artifacts—i.e., patronage. The Transition Team chairperson had an office next door to Spillane and, at times, was perceived as an ad-hoc executive assistant. This proved helpful as personnel inside and outside the central office "dropped by" to offer their views on what was happening. The Transition Team, then, provided critical information about personalities, interests and coalitions that existed so strategies could be developed.

The Legacy

The Boston School Department can be seen in two ways: the central office staff and the field staff. The central office staff included individuals at school headquarters. At the time of Spillane's arrival, these individuals numbered about 1,000 and included two deputy superintendents, five senior officers, administrators, supervisors, directors and support staff. Field staff included nine community superintendents, 123 principals and headmasters, approximately 5,200 teachers and 2,800 support staff.[1] Each of these staff made up the school organization and had its own personality. Spillane's dilemma in establishing management control meant knowing and responding to the peculiar personalities of each group.

The central office staff was comprised of "old-line employees" and "new faces." Old-line employees, who made up roughly 70 percent of the management personnel at school headquarters, trace their heritage back to the 1960's and early 1970's when school committees were dominated by white Irish Catholic incumbents. One university official pictured the school system this way: "He (Spillane) inherited an old school system that focused on patronage...there was no accountability; in fact, it was a non-accountability system." This gave rise to many independent areas of the school system that functioned like "fiefdoms." The pervasiveness of this system reached far into the bureaucracy and included federal project supervisors, custodians, school crossing guards, bus monitors and attendance officers. But the deepest pockets of patronage were in the critical areas of budget and personnel.

New faces trace their heritage to appointments made by superintendents in the mid and late 1970's. These superintendents, finding it difficult to replace old-line employees, opted for establishing their own bureaucracy based on a loyalty to them. The layers of bureaucracy, one school official noted, was "like an archeological dig." One former superintendent "gave up trying to penetrate the system so he built up his own system...he built a shadow organization to the right of the existing system."

New faces can also trace their heritage to a changing school committee that began to succumb to the affirmative action demands the Federal government placed on the school system. More blacks and minorities were hired in the four years preceding Spillane's appointment than during any other time in the recent history of the Boston Public Schools. These appointments gave way to an emerging pocket of black leadership that drew the strength from the court as well as from the black and minority community.

43

The field staff also included many old-line employees and new faces. Principals and headmasters, for example, enjoyed the safest tenure: "In Boston, if you were a principal, you usually died in that position or you were transferred by your own request." In some cases, much of this security was tied directly to a school committee member; in other cases, it was tied directly to the many neighborhoods that dot the landscape of Boston. A turf-conscious city, these principals (and other administrators) could rely on espousing the philosophy of the neighborhood to maintain their stability and job.

New faces also appeared in the field in the same way that they did at the central headquarters. Under one previous superintendent, district offices ballooned with new appointments that assured loyalty to the administration and met the mandates of a Federal court order for affirmative action.

This background created an urgency for Spillane to exert his authority and establish control. The school system was suffering from a "terminal illness...there were a lot of complications." A series of changes in leadership saw two superintendents and one acting superintendent come and go in the fourteen months prior to Spillane's arrival. No visible and stable leadership was evident to either the central office or community superintendents and principals in the districts. "It was a difficult situation; it made an already parochial system more defensive and bureaucratic and an easy target for would-be critics, who constantly attacked the schools...the public perception of the Boston schools was that of a whipping boy."

This state of siege led to a protective and defensive lethargy, and more often than not, "uncertainty reigned." For one observer, Spillane did not need to exert much effort to establish management control.

[Many were] tired...for the most part, they'd lay down their weapons for a new superintendent, a new leader...they were willing to work with him. They had been through so much that they were just tired...what they wanted most was leadership.

There was another reason why Spillane had to exert his authority but it was less subtle. "If you took a poll," commented one school official, "you'd find that more than 50 percent wanted the new superintendent to fail." Spillane realized this and quipped,

Some people want you to succeed because they'll have a place to work...others want you to fail because you'll expose their incompetence...and find out that they owe their job to someone...without any qualifications.

Those who wanted Spillane to fail became ardent "Spillane watchers." They exhibited two strategies. One strategy was a "quiet type of sabotage." "They'll just sit there, sit back and wait...they're not going to get too tough with him because they have a job; you've got to realize that they're not going to jeopardize that since, you know, the school system pays so well."

Even among the field staff, there was one philosophy that characterized some administrators: "At the school level, there is always a question of whether he'd be here for long...so why bother. You could survive better if you didn't identify with the new superintendent since it can be counter-productive so that when the next superintendent comes in you're not already labeled."

Three weeks after Spillane recommended the layoff of 1,070 teachers, he found 250 teachers who were on payroll but not on the payroll list. The payroll list was critical to the layoffs because it served to identify the least senior teachers who were slated for the layoffs. So in the middle of his first crisis (layoffs), Spillane "discovered 250 people slipped through the cracks." As a result, some teachers were mistakenly laid off. They had more seniority than those who were not laid off and on an appeal by the Boston Teachers Union, they were re-instated.

Such chaos can be attributed to the poor state of records kept by the personnel and budget office. Some school observers suggested that personnel problems were probably tolerated because "it was useful to keep this level of chaos since it made it easy to slip friends and relatives on the payroll and no one ever knew about it." Even Spillane recounted later that "the place is always planting land mines and banana peels where you least expect it."

Time to Act

Spillane responded to these organizational characteristics in a unique way. He did not impose on the organization a grand scheme for establishing management control. He responded to the organization by attacking specific weaknesses.

Spillane sent his first reorganization memorandum to the school committee on October 14, 1981, six weeks after starting the job. In that memo, he noted: "My observations and analysis indicate that it was extremely difficult...to affix responsibility and accountability...that departments and offices that should have been working together...were neither organizationally related to one another nor operationally communicating with one another...The organizational changes require no additional positions, merely a more logical assignment of responsibilities under newly defined Deputy Superintendents..."[2] In doing so, he placed responsibility and staff where he wanted and under the supervision he could trust.

Spillane made a two-person management operation into a three-person operation. The new Deputy Superintendent for School Operations assumed operational responsibilities formerly with the academic and management deputies. He became responsible for running the schools on a daily basis, including the coordination of school district and school level administrators. The new Deputy Superintendent for Curriculum and Instruction, relieved of operational matters, was responsible for curriculum planning and development. And, the Deputy Superintendent for Finance assumed all responsibility for financial and personnel matters, where once these were scattered and uncoordinated.

The finance position was especially important if Spillane was to establish management control over budget and personnel. This priority reflected his reorganization.

He gave budget management responsibilities to the Deputy Superintendent of Finance. And he gave the Deputy Superintendent for Finance "the responsibility for and authority over personnel management, budget development as well as...control over the access to the data management sources necessary for these units to have clear and updated personnel and budget figures."[3]

Establishing New Habits

Management control is more than a matter of being "clear and concise about how you're going to organize." It is a matter of staffing the organization with individuals who could do the job. Spillane resisted the urge to build his own bureaucratic structure as former superintendents had done. He did not employ a "new broom sweeps clean" philosophy nor arouse the central office with "mass firings." Instead, he fashioned a team from existing players and relied on outsiders for only a few key appointments. He "learned to live with people" and redirect their efforts. He also learned from the history of the organization that it was unwise to try to crack the layers of bureaucracy that cemented themselves in the structure of the organization. Rather than tackle the bureaucracy, he "fused the different layers together" under a new leadership. His approach was direct. "I told them I was going to clean up the mess and that meant looking at how the place ought to be...I said I was going to make re-appointments in the new structure and that while I am unhappy with the way they were running the operation...they could stay on if they thought they could do the job...but I reserve the right to hire new people (later)."

Key appointments reflected this staffing strategy. One appointment that Spillane made was the new Deputy Superintendent for Finance Operations, who came with Spillane from the New York State Department of Education. She was a window into the bureaucracy, a means by which he could "straighten out the financial mess." She was the leverage by which Spillane could control the patronage in the system. Some old-line staff in the budget management office were considered "sacred cows"; their dismissal could have caused a confrontation and diverted Spillane's attention from establishing management control. Instead he used the reorganization as a way to respect this heritage yet monitor the staff.

Spillane received two letters of resignation during his first week on the job; they were from Jim Walsh and Marcia Soden, administrative assistants under Acting Superintendent Joseph McDonough. He expected the resignations and so did Walsh and Soden who told him "he should have the right to pick his own administrative assistants and they were prepared to leave on his request." Characteristic of his style, Spillane told them he would not accept the resignations at this time: "Let's see how it goes and I'll let you know in sixty days."

Both appointments were important. Walsh, an old-line employee, could help Spillane interpret the history of the organization. "He knew everybody, where they came from and what they could do." He served as a window to that old-line staff that is part of every organization. It was a good move in another way, commented a former university official: "Jim could be the sergeant-at-arms for Spillane, take care of the ministerial duties and be his right hand man. But at the same time he did not have aspirations for the superintendency so there was no moral conflict with the advice he gave." Soden, on the other hand, was a new face in the organization, a young attractive black woman who could reach into the organization for perspectives that Walsh could not provide.

Spillane kept Robert Peterkin in a senior position by appointing him Deputy Superintendent for School Operations. Peterkin, a black, was a candidate for the job of superintendent. Nevertheless, Spillane reassigned him according to the new reorganization plan. He also replaced the Personnel Director with Ida White, a black. Both appointments represented his commitment to affirmative action.

He won school committee support for a new salary rating system and a new job classification policy. These changes created several new job titles for existing personnel and eliminated others, created new positions and boosted salaries for seventeen employees. One week later, Spillane followed with a recommendation to demote two of his five senior officials.

Key appointments and other staffing changes were critical for Spillane to gain control. The history sent signals that old-line staff were not going to be coerced into doing Spillane's will. If there was going to be a new direction, they would have to be involved. (Under the previous superintendent, who chose to build an organization alongside the existing structure, the old-line staff stone-walled directives and sabotaged initiatives.) Also, certain key appointments serve as windows on the organization. They see into the organization and provide an informal evaluation of the system.

In addition to those efforts, Spillane also focused on the field staff. He made a number of changes at the community superintendent level and the school site level. However, with the field staff, Spillane employed a different mind-set.

He was more direct with the bureaucratic layers built by former superintendents. He dismissed and reassigned more than 50 special staff assistants assigned to the nine community superintendents. In doing so, he revised the decentralization efforts of previous superintendents and brought control closer to his office. While this earned him the reputation as a "top-down" administrator, it nevertheless gave him the opportunity to influence management directives.

Spillane also did away with a long standing agreement with the Boston Association of School Administrators and Supervisors (BASAS). He learned of this agreement from a request by a principal who asked for an additional assistant principal. Spillane queried for a rationale and was told that the school district used targets to staff the schools and that for each 400 students there should be two assistant principals. When he pushed for the school's enrollment, Spillane found out it was 403.

Spillane changed the ratio soon after school opened in September so that 39 assistant principals were reassigned or transferred. "He took a tough stand on that," commented one school official; but at the same time he won plaudits for "cutting waste and attacking mismanagement."

Management control comes about by hiring new employees; but it also requires firing unproductive incumbents. The dismissal of employees sends signals to the organization that purpose exists and follow-up persists. The combination of these two actions also lends support to those who have been doing a good job and wish to continue to do so. Even Spillane's shake-up of the principals and changes in the central office included a number of promotions and transfers based on excellence of performance.

The heart of Spillane's management control efforts was his ability to quickly put in place a performance evaluation system that made accountability a reality and not a myth. All employees were evaluated. "Accountability must start at the top," he told a gathering of parents six weeks into the job noting that means administrators as well as teachers.[4]

What emerged was an evaluation documents for each of three classes of administrators—central and district office administrators, principals and headmasters and assistant principals and assistant headmasters. Each document was a simple four-page format that required a supervisor to rate an employee as unsatisfactory, satisfactory or exceptional.

Neither the central office nor field staff was formally evaluated. In fact "most evaluations were quite informal." The only evaluation document of record was a "little-used evaluation procedure for non-tenured teachers employed by the Federal court" which involved parents and community groups.

The effort provided a signal to employees that the ability to perform must be demonstrated. It gave Spillane's reorganization efforts strength and purpose even though it was criticized for the lack of input by staff and the brief training provided for using the documents. Still, according to one school employee, "the message was clear...the loss of a job created a real fear."

Spillane relied on this performance evaluation system to focus his reorganization and cement his control over the management of the school system. He relied on evaluations to demote and dismiss central office personnel and reshuffle field personnel.

Spillane demoted or dismissed 41 administrators on June 8, 1982. Then, in what was billed as the "largest administrative shake-up in the last three decades", Spillane announced on July 21 he reassigned 22 of the city's 123 principals and headmasters.[5] "There are some shifts because of my unhappiness with the leadership in those schools..." he commented. Others were more blunt. Carmen Pola, co-chairperson of the Citywide Parents Advisory Council said, "It's about time. It's long overdue." And, one school official confessed, "[He is] the first one to shake up the ranks of the principals...[whose] abilities ranged from marginal to superior." Many others told me this was the first step to affect change in the classroom.

Chapter 4
The Incident

Clear grade-by-grade curriculum objectives are being drawn up in the major academic areas (Reading/Language Arts, Mathematics, Science, and Social Studies), K–12 and distributed to all teachers, with explanatory material for parents. They contain maximum and minimum expectations.[1]

The Boston school system had published more than twenty curriculum guides in the ten years prior to Spillane's becoming superintendent. Many guides were written by the nine community school district offices in order to address their own needs. Each district went about "doing its own thing," and the school district was left without uniform standards for all students across the city.

Spillane's predecessor, Robert Wood, set in motion a plan to remedy the situation. He hired a black woman, Bernice Miller, as Director of the Office of Curriculum and Competency (OCC) to prepare a curriculum for the city's schools. However, one university official commented,

Spillane inherited a number of appointments, like Bea Miller…it was a definite leadership problem. Wood hired her because he was looking for black appointments…she and O'Bryant are close friends.[2]

Another school observer expressed it this way: "Back then (when Wood took over) the School Committee, instead of getting into policy, they got into personnel staffing…" These commentators, and others, suggested there was some personnel trading so that both the School

Committee and the Superintendent could develop and maintain leverage with a constituency.

Furthermore, the Federal court, supervising a desegregation order in the Boston Public Schools, imposed its will on the curriculum writing effort. Through a series of court orders, Miller and the OCC were instructed to develop a curriculum that reflected multi-cultural and multi-racial objectives. The court orders gave Miller and the OCC a measure of protection. By the time Spillane arrived, Miller had developed a base of power that rested on the court and her ties to John O'Bryant. One official noted this even caused Wood some problems: "Look what happened to Wood," he commented. "He came out publicly that the reading scores were improving in the school system...then Miller came out with a whole bunch of other statistics. That really made him (Wood) look bad."

The OCC spent two years meeting with teachers and curriculum area specialists to draft a curriculum—a set of school district curriculum objectives. The draft highlighted the specific teaching objectives for five content areas in grades K–8. It was written in order to establish a uniform teaching platform so that teachers knew what they were expected to teach; in short, it was a document of teacher expectations.

The draft went through serious criticism. The spring before Spillane arrived, the draft was submitted to Acting Superintendent Joseph McDonough. He quickly became uncomfortable with it saying it had enough grammatical and typographical errors in it "to damage its credibility in the schools." Still, he submitted it to the School Committee because "I felt the need was so great."[3]

The School Committee had not acted on it prior to Spillane's arrival. He, like McDonough, had problems with it. The OCC draft he noted, "was an embarrassment. I wouldn't put my name on it." While the work of the OCC (teacher meetings and study) was good, he added that the draft meant "someone had to break down all the jargon, the pedagese."[4] Miller defended herself by saying it was always "Hurry up and get it done...which prompted among ourselves a certain amount of grousing because we were getting more to do than we planned."[5]

Spillane needed a curriculum document that he could deliver to parents and was easily understood by them. This meant a set of grade-by-grade student expectations that stated: "Students at each grade level will be able to do…" He was trying to avoid the mystery that surrounded previous curriculum efforts. He needed a document that could serve as a set of targets for the staff. With specific criteria established as uniform standards, all schools could be held accountable for the success or failure of their students. This was important to him in order to exercise his management authority over the diverse make-up of the 123 schools in the Boston Public Schools.

Spillane's discussions with Miller focused on getting a draft that met his specifications and brought to light a difference in philosophy about the substance and purpose of the draft. The discussions were not new to Miller and the OCC staff. The year before, McDonough tried to move the OCC curriculum in the direction of grade-by-grade student expectations and had been stoutly resisted by the OCC staff.[6] Spillane found the same resistance.

Spillane met with Miller during the first month; but as he reflected, "she didn't want to do it my way." The tension increased over this time. The OCC document, which concentrated on multi-cultural objectives, was responsive to a minority school population. Miller argued that earlier standards did not reflect this make-up of the Boston Public Schools. The two also differed over the degree to which the curriculum should be both a management tool as well as an instructional standard.

The argument over philosophical differences became a confrontation. Spillane commented, "I had to fight Miller…she was actually going away from here saying she'll do what she wants to do; that no one will tell her. So, it's really having the guts to say 'Look, I'm the Superintendent, I run the show…take it or leave it.'"

"It was like a street fight," commented one school official. "It was a direct confrontation…like who's running the show." As a result, the curriculum writing effort became a management issue. Over the subsequent three months it also prompted a fight with John O'Bryant over administrative authority and raised doubts about Spillane's radical sensitivity.

Rather than wait for these philosophical differences to be resolved, Spillane ordered that the curriculum draft be re-written and assigned

Kim Marshall, a former (white) teacher, as special assistant to do it under his direction. Miller and her staff objected. Miller's black assistant, Betty Bryant, who was responsible for preparing the draft, pressed her case in a memo to Spillane on October 2. In the memo, she complained about the appointment of Marshall to re-write the curriculum instead of herself and sent copies of the memo to the School Committee.

Spillane asked for Bryant's resignation. He put it to me this way when I spoke with him the day he sent the letter: "I can't sit still, there's too much to do. I just asked for a resignation…this woman (Bryant) wrote me a letter and I didn't like the tone. I didn't demand a letter of resignation but suggested she could write me one at her convenience and drop it on my desk."

Observers I spoke with saw Spillane's effort as essentially exercising the right to delegate responsibilities to certain staff members. They said Spillane felt that senior officials are "his people." "Anyone on that floor (Superintendent offices) are his people and serve at his pleasure." One school official commented, however, that the issue

> caused him a lot of grief. Even McDonough tried to get rid of that person. I think what he did was say "I'll just do it. I'll take the heat but work around it and eventually everything will get back to normal."

Things did not get back to normal; the issue intensified and became a complicated administrative authority issue involving School Committee President, John D. O'Bryant. One school observer saw it this way: "The incident opened up a situation for O'Bryant and Miller to say 'OK, let's get him,' so the charges of racism came out."

O'Bryant waited until after his November re-election to the School Committee to defend the OCC and criticize Spillane. It was a politically astute move. Receiving the largest number of votes of any other School Committee candidate, O'Bryant pushed his case in a November 12 memo to Spillane. He termed Spillane's reassignment of curriculum writing as "arbitrary and impulsive" and chastised Spillane for asking for Bryant's resignation. Referring to Marshall's work, O'Bryant said, "You don't re-write curriculum for 60,000 kids by one person…so he's written a couple of books, big deal."[7] O'Bryant also called Spillane's handling of the curriculum situation an embarrassment to Miller and the OCC staff.

The media exposed O'Bryant's disagreement with Spillane and stirred debate that their relationship had become strained. One school observer close to both men noted,

O'Bryant and Spillane...yeah, image was important to both of them. Both men see what they say in the newspaper. I mean Spillane's image was very important...Me, I just go by the mirror but Spillane stops to see if it's all in place. O'Bryant's the same way...this is evident when you speak to them.

For Spillane, the issue focused on administrative authority: the right to dismiss senior officials. But for O'Bryant, the issue encompassed a broader importance. Three school observers noted that O'Bryant wanted "to bring in more blacks, but there was no way to do that with the lack of dollars and the cutbacks at the central office. So it was important to keep who he had...Miller was a close friend and she was seen as one of the people to protect." Even the media inferred this scenario.

O'Bryant vehemently objected to the comments in the paper that suggested black patronage was behind the squabble with Spillane. On one occasion, O'Bryant called a meeting with the editorial board of one leading newspaper to voice his objection to their inferences. "He (O'Bryant) was bullshit," commented one school official. "I think what really ticked him off was the comment that he was playing the Irish role."

Spillane and O'Bryant met soon after the November 12 memo to open up the lines of communication. The meeting was described as amicable, but O'Bryant pressed his case in the subsequent interview. "He's the chief executive officer, he can do what he wants," O'Bryant remarked. "But we (the School Committee) don't have to accept it. We have a highly paid staff. I hope it's not wasted."[8]

Spillane made short shrift of this accommodation with O'Bryant. He decided not to press for Bryant's dismissal but also kept Marshall working on re-writing the curriculum. On November 18, he sent a memo to the School Committee in order to defend his actions that some felt embarrassed Miller and the OCC. In the memo, he noted the draft proposal he received was full of jargon and unsuited for use in the public schools. He went on to say it was "riddled with bureaucratese such as articulated differentiated body parts" which neither parents, teachers—and particularly pupils—could possibly recognize as clear understandable English. He criticized individual sections saying that the draft included "itty bitty reading skills" and on page 2, item 7 of his memo, he said that the mathematics section "had been lifted with a few word changes from the Hong Kong schools."[9]

I was curious why Spillane would make such comments. He replied,

I defended myself with what I had to do. It was not a ruse. Actually, it was really true...I knew how it was written. It took them two years, that's true but I had it on absolute authority that my statements were true.

When I pressed him on this point, he added,

The peer (OCC) assigned to write it (under Bryant), he was part of the issue. Even the blacks in the department told me the process...I confronted them...the person actually took the Hong Kong guide home (a British School System) and re-wrote it. He was Chinese...it became a racial slur against the Chinese.

The memo became public, and the Citywide Parents Advisory Council lost no time in reacting. In a letter to Spillane, published by the *Boston Herald American*, CPAC pointed particularly at item 7.

This statement not only denigrates the staff at the Office of Curriculum and Competency but, more dangerously, expresses a racist attitude on your part...it can only be interpreted as a direct insult to the Chinese Community...As the Superintendent of a public school system under court-ordered desegregation...you have the responsibility and obligation to be most sensitive to racial and cultural issues...The taxpayers are not paying you $50,000 a year to be thoughtless and insulting to anyone.[10]

The racial commentary intensified and brought an uncomfortable dimension to the administrative authority issue. One university official noted,

It was a tactical mistake to hire Marshall (a white aide) to re-write the curriculum...he's going to have tremendous difficulty, maybe a scar...that he'll carry for quite a while.

Spillane, reflecting on the move conceded,

You know hindsight is better...like taking away curriculum writing from Miller (and Bryant). It turned out to be a black versus white thing...and the quotes helped to get everyone into the act.

The quotes also helped to increase the criticism that he was racially insensitive. It prompted people to say what they were thinking, that Spillane's dismissal of a black and appointment of a white was racially motivated. "It really gave bad vibes among the black community," commented one black leader. "We know hundreds of examples of incompetent administrators—closet administrators. But why did he choose this person, a black?"

The squabble, or fight as some called it, lost momentum but never disappeared. It came back to haunt Spillane when he sought a four-year contract from the School Committee in March, 1982. Indeed, the curriculum incident was one of four key issues that Spillane had to address and resolve to the consideration of the black school committee members if they were going to vote favorably on his contract.

Spillane dropped his case against Miller and the OCC, but he kept the responsibility for re-writing the curriculum. He reflected,

It was a tradeoff...my tangle with John O'Bryant also kept me able to have a curriculum going. I was able to keep my aide working on the curriculum. If I didn't do that then we wouldn't have a curriculum...for sure. I knew what I wanted to do and I didn't back down...it's my turf so I didn't back off.

Chapter 5
Blue Books and Red Books

Joseph M. McDonough, one of Boston's seven school superintendents in the last nine years, walks around a long folding table and points to the 40 [curriculum] books spread out like unmatched dishes at a pot-luck supper. There are red books and blue books, thick books and thin books, book bound by plastic spirals and books bound by staples...The books represent 16 years of work...One book...that education specialists say is most essential for an urban school system is missing: a modern, uniform city-wide curriculum that sets a consistent course of instruction in basic skills for each grade.[1]

The last curriculum guide published by the Boston School Department was in 1969. It took its place alongside the other guides that symbolized a system that "encouraged disparate and disconnected curriculums—some written for individual classrooms, some for specific schools, some for certain districts but discouraged...[a] uniform city-wide curriculum."[2]

Much of the "curriculum anarchy"[3] that existed could be traced to the philosophy of previous superintendents and Federal court intervention into the educational practices of the school department. As early as 1972 and continuing through until Spillane's tenure, curriculum development was a decentralized activity. Many of the central office functions associated with curriculum (staff development) were moved from the central office to the nine community districts in the city. Boosted by large sums of Federal aid, these community districts built their own curriculum departments that wrote and published localized curriculum guides. The

59

result was not that curriculum was relegated to a second, third, or fourth priority for school committees but that, as Spillane said, "it didn't have a place."

Even the Federal court encouraged this decentralization of curriculum activity. For the court, it represented an effort to bring the control of instruction closer to the black and non-black minority clients of the system.

This curriculum disparity did not keep pace with the needs of a changing school clientele. As a result, a "politics of curriculum" emerged—i.e., different groups pressed for curriculum revision for different reasons. One educational authority put it this way:

If you didn't have a city-wide curriculum to go by...you have a standard of progress that obtains in one part of the city and not in another, or a standard of progress that obtains for black and not for whites, or for Hispanics and not for blacks.[4]

In short, there was a call for a centralized effort that projected a multi-ethnic and multi-racial focus that could not be left to the dictates of community districts.

A *Boston Globe* article entitled "The Other Segregation in City Schools," noted the economic and social characteristics of this school clientele:

...overall, 40% of the city school students come from families receiving welfare; according to some estimates more than half the students in the schools live in public housing. More than half the students in the schools are eligible for free hot lunches...In sum, Boston's schools are predominantly the schools of the poor and near poor. They have been abandoned by middle-income families of all races.[5]

This change in the clientele made a uniform city-wide curriculum a necessity. One school official noted "so many of the kids in the schools today come from families that may move two or three times in a school year. If a kid isn't able to fit right into a new class, the whole year will be lost to him."[6] The Transition Report is more specific: "Students who moved from one school to another (a frequent event in the years of desegregation) often found not only different textbooks and materials, but entirely different curriculum objectives."[7]

The parents sending their children to school were not the only ones who had a vested interest in a city-wide curriculum. The business community and the Mayor had a stake in a city-wide curriculum. The business community, chastised by others for turning "a cold shoulder" to the schools, had a poor image in the city. They needed a city-wide curriculum that would reverse the "dismal quality of the product of the schools evidenced by a large dropout rate." They could then begin to look in a city schools for a labor supply rather than in the larger metropolitan area. In addition, the business community needed a skilled labor force to prepare for its own growth. One businessman commented, "The business community saw growth and even planned for it but there wasn't an equivalent growth in training at the schools to meet the needs we had or were planning to have."

Also, Mayor White was often caught in the middle. On one hand, his own constituency attacked the schools for their poor performance and image; this made him reluctant to support the schools and provide needed additional funds. On the other hand, he was criticized by school parents and school organizations for "abandoning the schools."

The political necessity for a city-wide curriculum bent on meeting the needs of certain groups as well as providing quality education can be seen from another perspective. Over a ten year period, from 1970 to 1980, more than 35,000 students left the system to attend private schools. Spillane noted,

> *We have witnessed an outflow of 35,000 students from the Boston Public Schools in the past ten years, almost 40% of the 95,000 in 1972. There is no exodus from the city or birth decline to account for that sort of drop....Last year (1980–81) 18,000 were in parochial and 2,000 were in private schools inside city limits, while another 10,000 went to parochial and private schools outside the city.*[8]

Many parents I interviewed talked in terms of political support for the schools and the need to encourage students to return to the Boston Public Schools. A parent leader summarized it this way.

People left in droves...and it just seemed to get worse...people leaving, then schools closed which brought more disruption because of the teacher layoffs...[but] there is a middle class in the city and their kids are not in the schools...they'd come back...and would be grateful to the Superintendent if they knew he could get something for the kids.

The need to develop a city-wide curriculum was politically as well as instructionally motivated. "He had to do it," advised one school official; "if he didn't get that [city-wide] curriculum published it would have been damaging." The Chairman of the Transition Team agreed. He found that Spillane was sensitive to the political implication of a city-wide curriculum. He noted "at first Spillane said he needed help...there were lots of issues...but the more we met the more he was concerned with a city-wide curriculum."

But whatever effort Spillane made, it still would not be enough to produce significant results. One year could not produce a structure to assure "consistency over the system, so that a student can switch schools without losing his way academically..."[9] Nor could one year solve an inordinately high truancy rate or prevent more than three out of every ten high school students from dropping out of school.[10] Likewise, one year was not enough time to skillfully redesign the curriculum so that the Boston Public Schools could assure graduates an opportunity for full-time employment in the city's business environment.

What Spillane had to do was make people believe that the school system was headed in the right direction and that these problems could be solved. It was important to develop confidence in the school system.[11] One school official said it this way:

While he was asking what can we do with less bucks, surfacing in the background was quality education and accountability. His response was to write the curriculum. Every kid in every grade level spelled out to parents...it put him in a very advantageous position. Parents could now believe that their kids would be able to go into one school and pick up where they left off.

Setting the Tone

The Boston Public Schools had not had a top-down, system-wide redesign of curriculum goals since 1969. Spillane addressed this issue. Instead of directing energies at a massive curriculum effort, he published a comprehensive list of city-wide objectives which he called the "core curriculum." These were "clear grade-by-grade curriculum objectives...in the major academic subjects (Reading/Language Arts, Mathematics, Science and Social Studies) K–12...[which] contained maximum and minimum expectations of students."[12] It was clear to Spillane that mandating city-wide objectives was not the same as mandating a city-wide curriculum.

The objectives approach could be a signal to the clients of the system and something he could do in his first year that could lay the foundation for curriculum efforts in later years.

The objectives approach also reflected his own thinking. While Deputy Commissioner of Elementary and Secondary Schools for New York State, he pushed for minimum graduation requirements for all high school students. This got him into a squabble with Frank Macchiarola, chancellor of New York City Public Schools. Macciarola argued that first a curriculum must be established and then student objectives developed based on that curriculum. Still, as others found, "He (Spillane) came with a basic approach in his mind."

It decentralized curriculum efforts but in a way that was different from previous decentralization efforts. It brought the focus (power) for deciding what should be taught back to the central office. It brought policy making back to the central office while leaving the schools with implementation rights. Spillane commented, "...the role of the central curriculum office is not to impose methods and material on teachers...the responsibility for developing the most effective, responsive, and creative teaching methods and materials to meet student needs—and tap teacher strengths—should rest squarely on teachers and principals..."[13]

This approach laid the foundation for implementing an accountability program at all levels of the school system. Now the staff could be held accountable because there was something to hold them accountable. In his policy proposal, Spillane noted, "The central office should give a clear message to the schools: Here are the things your students should be able to do at the end of each year…"[14]

The accountability system spread the breadth of the school system. Spillane told the Council of Urban Boards of Education at a NSBA Convention that "Community Superintendents are held accountable for proper evaluation of headmasters and principals within their districts, and insuring that headmasters and principals are effectively implementing the evaluation process with teachers in their building."[15]

Based on this evaluation program, Spillane, at the end of the school year, fired two non-tenured teachers. He recommended that four tenured teachers (one with 20 years of experience in the system) be dismissed and ten others be placed on probation. Spillane noted, this served as a signal "that lack of professionalism and incompetence will not be tolerated."[16]

Spillane relied on the city-wide objectives so that teachers and principals could be held accountable for a clear set of academic expectations tied directly to student achievement. He backed up the objectives with city-wide competency tests so that "they are taken seriously by teachers; without such tests, teachers who have grown accustomed to their own private curriculums might well ignore the new objectives."[17]

But the competency tests, as a support system for teacher and administrative accountability, also served as a support system for the staff.

Backing It Up

The competency tests served as a way of measuring student progress and getting detailed information about the students in order to make instructional decisions at the school level. "Otherwise, each teacher will operate in a vacuum and, despite individual heroics, the overall program will not be effective."[18]

In addition to the competency tests, Spillane developed a promotional policy. Aimed at preventing students from sliding from year to year, the policy set up promotional standards from grade to grade so that "teachers could have some confidence that students entering their classrooms would have certain prerequisite skills and knowledge."[19] This effort signaled a commitment to instructional standards and carried with it a "back-to-the-basics" appeal for a majority of the city's population.

If the first job that Spillane had, in the curriculum sense, was to improve the quality of education available to students in the Boston Public Schools, then the second job was to insure a safe environment for these students to learn.

In November he spoke candidly about violence in the schools and his plan for dealing with it. He ordered "that any student who commits any act of violence on another student or adult, or who is found in possession of a dangerous weapon, shall be immediately suspended, under due process, from the regular school program." The number of suspensions and discipline hearings increased. Students who returned to school after a suspension were reassigned to self-contained teaching areas for specific periods of time before returning to the regular program.

Spillane was criticized for his stand on violence and discipline. A state-wide advocacy group call the suspension policy racist since the group found that the disparity between black and white suspensions was the highest in five years. He responded by saying he would continue his efforts and "spare no effort to insure that the schools are safe."[20]

These efforts culminated in a city-wide Code of Discipline published in April, 1982. The Code of Discipline, the work of a 20-member committee, ordered suspension for acts of violence as well as cutting class, sexual harassment, and so on.

But the real impact of the efforts to curb violence and a support system for discipline in the schools was seen in the following year. Kathleen Kelley, president of the Boston Teachers Union commented,

> *One of the reasons things have changed from last year is the discipline emphasis...that has increased morale. It was a key issue...it was the first time that the teachers and principals saw strength from the top, that central office would back us up...For example, last year I spent a lot of time in the middle schools and thought there were days the teachers were not going to make it...one school was at a point that they didn't allow children to move from classroom to classroom, instead teachers moved. It was instituted out a sense of survival...that has changed...teachers are all out in corridors this year...that has an effect on the schools.*

Kelley's comment points out that there is a link between curriculum efforts and discipline. Spillane saw the link and used his management prerogatives to institute centralized control over discipline in city schools. And he sought to do more. He sought to signal to two segments of the community that the political issue of confidence in the schools was a central priority on his agenda. One segment of the community was those who left the public schools. He believed that certain percentage of this unrelenting decline was due to parental fears for their children's safety.

Another segment of the population was those who had no children in the schools. They had little stake in the schools except to see that they reflected traditional values. Spillane's efforts were another way to appeal to this constituency. Accountability struck an accord with them because it said that the school system was simply getting the staff to do the job that the taxpayers were paying them to do. Likewise, Kelley noted, Spillane's discipline efforts "played well to this constituency who saw the Boston Public Schools as a blackboard jungle...and played well in neighborhoods because they saw him as someone who could bring students in line."

Setting It Up

Spillane remodeled the curriculum services at the central office to support these initiatives. They represented a new thinking.

The new structure separated the key components for the delivery of curriculum services and placed them under different authorities. The evaluation function, tied intimately to the performance evaluation of teachers and principals, was seen as an operations matter and became the responsibility of the Deputy Superintendents for Operations. It evaluated individuals on the basis of whether the "core" curriculum, or mandatory set of city-wide objectives, was being met.

The monitoring functions became the responsibility of the newly created position of Deputy Superintendent for Curriculum and Instruction. This new role offered a programmatic dimension to the senior staff where formerly it was dispersed the length and breadth of the system. This position centralized responsibility and provided "...greater direction and coordination in curriculum development and instructional support efforts, more effective integration of Bi-lingual, Special Education and funded programs within the core curriculum, and more effective approaches in areas such as competency standards, promotion policies and advanced class work."[21] This office also revitalized efforts to provide an effective staff development training program.

The new structure clearly spelled out who was responsible for the delivery of curriculum services that had been "somewhat of a mystery in previous years since it was written at the central office as well as in the districts." It gave Spillane quick access to remedy weaknesses that confronted him. It provided substantial authority over dealing with abuses in special education. These abuses were the focus of a 100-page report prepared by a court-appointed monitor assigned to examine special education practices in the Boston Public Schools. The report, published in March, found that a disproportionate number of minority students were placed in special education programs.

These efforts also reflected "a major change in the way central office administrators thought about curriculum in the last decade."[22] The new structure emphasized that the key responsibility of the central office was support for curriculum efforts at the school level. In a speech to the Phi Delta Kappan Society at Harvard University, Spillane said,

> *The promulgation of...a core curriculum is the proper function of the central office; but there are other curriculum functions which belong at the school level. Curriculum I is the core, the mandatory set of expectations of students at every grade level, backed up by competency tests. Curriculum II consists of the methods and materials teachers use to get the core across to their students. I feel that decisions on Curriculum II are best handled by those closest to the students—teachers and principals—rather than being mandated from the central or district offices."*[23]

This thinking made the schools answerable to Spillane. The purpose was to improve the quality of education as well as restore confidence in the Boston Public Schools. Spillane wanted to focus his efforts (accountability) on particularly one individual—the principal. He noted,

The key individuals in the school system, with regard to accountability, are the headmasters and principals. The system must begin to move toward more authority and autonomy for these leaders. In response to this concern, we are now designing procedures which will allow them to be more involved with budget development and staff selections.[24]

Making Sure It Works

The management vehicle Spillane used to focus these curriculum efforts—in particular, accountability—was an approach called School-based Management. The approach would "place increased authority in the hands of the school principals and...would hold them accountable for the achievement by students in particular schools: test results, student attendance, drop out rates and the like."[25] He was more direct about it in an address he gave to the Officers of Large City Administrator Associations.

Where, the public wants to know, is that simple little sign, the buck stops here? And why isn't it on the most important desks in the school system, those of the building principals...there are principals in Boston who have turned schools around despite the bureaucratic mess. This tells me that there is a lot principals can do right now, even before structural and contractual changes are made.[26]

Spillane's plan for implementing School-based Management rested on the principals having more authority and autonomy in areas such as curriculum, budget and staffing. This meant he had to correct the deformities in the bureaucratic structure. However, it was more difficult to contend with contractual impediments and judicial mandates: "seniority and race could no longer be the sole criteria by which staff are assembled. Principals would have to be empowered to hire and fire teachers, to judge applicants based on evaluations of their credentials and performance."[27]

In December, 1981, Spillane convened a Work Group to plan a School-based Management project.[28] The group defined and elaborated on issues to be tested in the project: role of central and district offices, budget control at the school level, parent and community involvement in

68

decision making. Key goals were generated for a four-year project and the criteria for selecting pilot schools established. An intensive training program was set up and a plan for providing technical assistance and support identified.

Seven pilot schools were selected to participate in the school management project for the 1982–83 school year. The project meant hundreds of individuals would now become intimately involved with the management of the school system through school site councils. The councils were composed of parents, community representatives, teachers, and students and established to advise on subjects such as budgeting, curriculum and school discipline. This was important not only for later support of the project, but because it signaled an effort to build confidence in the schools. One parent commented that previously

> *all we [could] do is make recommendations and they [would] go up, up, up to Court Street…and then get lost on the way back down.*[29]

The effort was also meant to develop confidence among those parents who abandoned the school system. A parent organizer noted "most [parents] in my neighborhood send their kids to parochial schools…they need to feel some sort of control…they are not convinced that they could have some control in the schools, if they did, they'd come back."

The project still maintained an emphasis on school level authority even though some principals were dubious. "Many [said] nothing will happen…[and] that [we] can't hide behind the fact that [we] are still not in control of things," commented one principal.[30] Others were more optimistic. Another principal thought "it gave principals a feeling that [we] could make decisions and do the job…being a principal used to be a prestigious position and people respected it…it's a good effort at reform."

Chapter 6
A Shadow in My Mirror

On June 21, 1974, U.S. District Court Judge W. Arthur Garrity, Jr., found in Tallulah Morgan et al., Plaintiffs, v James W. Kerrigan et al., Defendants that the Boston School Committee had

> *violated the constitutional rights of plaintiff's class; that school authorities had knowingly carried out a systematic program of segregation affecting all of the city's students, teachers and school facilities and had intentionally brought about or maintained a dual system; that the entire school system of Boston was unconstitutionally segregated.*[1]

Angry Voices, 1974–1980

Judge Garrity ordered in 1974 that the school superintendent and School Committee comply with the Massachusetts' State Board of Education Racial Balance Plan for the 1974–75 school year and prepare and submit a plan of its own by December 16, 1974 for implementation in the 1975–76 school year.

The interim plan (1974–75 school year) was least restrictive since it was based on the State's Racial Imbalance Act that "defined school balance in a twisted way: Any public school was racially balanced if it contained 50 percent to 100 percent white students."[2]

The School Committee refused to implement the state's plan for the 1974–75 school year because it meant busing students to schools in line with racial quotas. Instead, Judge Garrity adopted the state's plan and ordered the school department to make the necessary preparations for September 12, 1974, the opening day of school.

Estimates indicated that nearly 20,000 students out of a total of 87,000 students would have to be bused. School protests and demonstrations plagued late summer plans for the opening of school. These carried over into the school year and especially at South Boston High School, the resolute symbol of a staunch white Irish Catholic neighborhood affectionately called Southie. At least two school committee members traced their heritage to "Southie" and took up the resistance to desegregation that eventually made Southie the symbol for the legions of anti-busing demonstrators.

It was against this background that the School Committee rejected a permanent desegregation plan prepared by its own staff during the fall (1974). They failed to meet the December 16 deadline set by the court. Three school committee members (who voted against the plan) were held in contempt of court. In response, Judge Garrity appointed two court experts to advise him in the preparation of a plan for desegregating the Boston Public Schools. Eventually this task fell to a Panel of Masters who were charged by judge Garrity to study the evidence and recommend "a plan meeting constitutional standards..."[3] The plan was readied for the opening of the 1975–76 school year and soon was dubbed "Judge Garrity's Plan."[4]

The plan, essentially the one that Spillane inherited, committed the school system to busing as a remedy to segregation. The commitment to busing provided the basis for a thorough restructuring of the school system. The plan created eight community school districts and one city-wide magnet school district.

These community school districts were pivotal to the restructuring scheme. Dentler and Scott note, "The eight districts were arrived at inductively by measuring facilities, distances between residential locales and schools, student diversities, ethnic distributions, and historic dimensions of neighborhoods within [the community school district]."[5]

Student assignments, the most controversial aspect of the plan, were based on geocodes. A geocode is a smaller unit within the community school district "comprising several blocks of real estate."[6] The use of geocodes was borrowed from the police department system to communicate the location of calls for radio patrol cars. The school department bought the geocode maps to facilitate their planning. More than 800 geocodes served as the basis for student assignments and the notion was "to assign clusters of geocode units within each school district to particular schools...by ethnicity and grade level."[7] So significant and sensitive were these geocodes that most of Judge Garrity's orders in the year following the adoption of the plan were issued to assure its credible implementation.

The geocodes served as a basis for producing racially balanced schools and implementing the standard set by the plan: the ethnic composition in each school in a district should not vary by more than 25 percent of the ethnic composition of the student population in the whole district. Only two districts—East Boston and Dorchester—were allowed to deviate beyond the 25 percent variance due to unusual residential settlements.

The plan also called for "pairing schools with businesses, universities and cultural institutions to support, assist and participate in the development of educational excellence within and among the public schools of Boston";[8] established a uniform grade structure among districts that included grades kindergarten through five for elementary schools, grades six through eight in middle schools and nine through twelve in high schools; recommended bi-lingual programs of instruction throughout the city in order to assure compliance with state bi-lingual education laws; and, established bi-racial parent councils for each district and every school and a Citywide Parents Advisory Committee (CPAC) to coordinate these councils, monitor school desegregation, and advise the court.

By the opening of school in 1975–76, white student enrollment dropped by 8,500, or nearly 10 percent. The reaction to busing was severe and eventually found its way into the schools. One school official recollected,

Fire, mayhem, fights...these were on the edges and eventually found their way into the schools...people thought of the schools as anti-schools...they really became non-schools...you just don't send kids there.

School Committee recalcitrance continued. "It was grandstanding at its best" remembered one parent, "that time with busing…the School Committee would keep getting up saying we will never tolerate busing…those school committees came in with their own agendas." Finally, in December, 1975, Judge Garrity placed South Boston High School, the symbol of resistance to busing and where violent acts and crimes were underscored in the media, under court receivership. Garrity ordered administrative staff and several teachers transferred because serious uncooperative attitudes had fostered segregation.[9]

Judge Garrity also used other judicial resources to affect a remedy for the segregation he found in the Boston Public Schools. He appointed a steady stream of "experts" to advise him on implementing the court's plan. He relied on "court monitors" to assess the development of specific aspects of the plan such as bi-lingual education. These individuals served as quasi-administrative officials and eventually underscored the polarization of management between the school system and the court. Their suggestions and advice became the basis for the numerous court orders that Judge Garrity issued to focus his implementation of the desegregation order.

Over the course of the next six years, Judge Garrity issued more than 200 orders to buttress the Boston School Desegregation Plan. These extended the reach of the plan into vital management areas and focused the court's involvement for Spillane. Transportation route were added and deleted to accommodate student assignments. Safety and security procedures were established that bound policy making at the school department offices, and teacher and administrative desegregation standards were set so that 20 percent of the staff (with a goal of 25 percent) were blacks or other minorities. For teacher and administrative desegregation, court orders spelled out the procedures for screening candidates for permanent positions as well as evaluating administrators in each of the nine districts. Court orders also established the Department of Implementation to oversee student assignments and hastened the design of an Affirmative Action Office.

Who Governs?

This background highlights how a Federal court can infiltrate the day-today operations and intervene into the management of a school system. These intrusions create a composite that is unique to an urban school superintendent and one that impacted Spillane's tenure. In Boston, it created an external constituency that he had to confront; it created an internal constituency that he had to address; and, it created sub-systems within the organization that he could not control.

The external constituency that Spillane had to work with was the Citywide Parents Advisory Council (CPAC). Predominantly minority parents, this group spearheaded much of the court's efforts to legitimize black and minority rights. They acted as an oversight agency that could influence the school site as well as draw attention to policy-making at school headquarters.

These advocates of desegregation were established by the court, and their mission and authority were spelled out by court orders; to monitor school desegregation, help improve race relations, and advise the court. They were supported by an annual budget of $500,000, drawn from school department funds as mandated by the court.

CPAC became recognized as an important vehicle for public participation in the schools; it served as the focus of a racially defined community participation effort established by the court for venturing into the management of the school system. The court established an elaborate system for the selection of principals and headmasters in order to break up the "old boy" network.[10] Similarly, the court designed and implemented a system of evaluations that relied on parent participation to monitor the practices of principals and headmasters. Much of this increased the already vivid intransigence school site officials had shown toward minorities in the past and made Spillane's efforts to comply with the court order more difficult. "You got to realize," commented one parent leader, "that I knew those principals (in certain neighborhoods)...they would tell me things and just assume because of my last name that I would feel the same way...there was some real evidence of racism at that level."

The court also legitimized the role of certain groups such as the Bi-Lingual Masterpac, established by the State to oversee the implementation of bi-lingual education for non-black minorities (Chinese, Hispanic). The roster of leaders in Bi-Lingual Masterpac is strikingly similar to that of CPAC, which gives credence to the court's narrow focus on parent participation. The new emerging parent leadership which Spillane inherited worked from two bases of authority; and each was a center for highlighting the racial issue facing the school system. Hispanics could also turn to the aggressive El Comite, a council of Hispanic parents and educators.

This network highlighted the importance of race in planning priorities and especially in defining who were the clients of the school system. While the plaintiffs in the Boston School Desegregation Case were black, other non-black minorities pushed for a role in the school system and were even joined to the case as "interveners." By the time Spillane became superintendent, the Hispanic El Comite had joined the black plaintiffs in a common cause. As a coalition, they pushed for multi-cultural and multi-ethnic programs that could not escape Spillane's attention when he set out to reform the curriculum. This network also represented rich possibilities for School Committee members. By 1978, the first black in more than 100 years was elected to the School Committee. In 1981, when Spillane took office, a Hispanic minority came close to unseating an incumbent white member. He found his new School Committee, which took office in January of his first year, pushing priorities that reflected minority interests which, at the same time, competed with other managerial and financial priorities he set for the first year.

The court also created and legitimized an internal constituency that Spillane had to address. In much the same way that the court used its authority to desegregate the student population, it also established measures to desegregate the teaching and administrative staff. Dentler and Scott note,

> All hiring of regular [staff] would occur on a one-to-one basis, one black to one white, until at least 20 percent of the permanent teacher force was black. And every building would contain a proportionate share of black teachers.[11]

At the teacher level, numbers were important. When Spillane became superintendent, he was committed to hiring at the teacher level so that he preserved the 20 percent mandate. One school official noted that "this sometimes caused some serious problems in trying to hire qualified white as well as black candidates for specific programs." When Spillane was confronted with a massive layoff in his first month, the same percentage had to guide his decision.

At the administrative level, it was more than numbers; it was a matter of position and influence. One black school official noted,

> *In terms of appointments, let's face it, white people control the administrative ranks…the student population is black but the staff is not…the court order addressed this issue. What are black educators concerned about?…we've paid our dues…got the degrees…now we want to be part of the system with key appointments in policy making positions…yeah, we were hoping for a black superintendent but we're willing to accept that will come…definitely want deputy superintendent…so when he made black appointments to those positions, it made him look favorable, gave him some credibility with the black community.*

The appointment of blacks to senior positions was important: "Those first moves in a racial climate…they've got to be in the right area and be the right person." One astute observer I interviewed pointed out that intangibles included a number of things.

> *[When he came]…the minority community was dissatisfied. The court laid the groundwork but former appointments were just to look good on paper…in reality, black people have got to be involved…what is clear is that you've got to play the game as a political player but you don't win the game by building an infrastructure that doesn't show up for ten years…*

Another observer is more direct.

> *He (a black appointment) had a position in the school's central office and even had some support in the black network…but lost it…so here the question was how many jobs have you gotten for black educators…what did he do to make black school committee members look good.*

The most apparent manifestation of the court's initiatives to desegregate the staff was the emergence of a black leadership in the internal structure of the organization. An important part of that black leadership was John O'Bryant, the first black school committee member since the Reconstruction period. As a member, and then as President of the School Committee, O'Bryant precariously balanced educational priorities with a determination to preserve black and minority interests. Another important part of the black leadership was the CPAC. The CPAC had a much wider network of influence than any other parent group and could call upon "thousands of otherwise uninvolved or excluded minority parents."[12] In fact, the slate of candidates that ran for School Committee election midway during Spillane's first year was sprinkled with minority aspirants, a first in the recent history of School Committee elections. The existing black administrators at the central office and in the school districts was another important part of the black leadership.

The network that emerged was often referred to as the "O'Bryant network" and it was this network that Spillane inherited when he took the job as superintendent. Black appointments were usually referred to in terms of whether or not they belonged to this network. This network was a growing concern to superintendents ever since it surfaced with the election of O'Bryant to the School Committee in 1978.

To many people I interviewed, this network meant visible appointments of black professionals at key central office positions. Some observers thought this gave a new meaning to patronage. One school official commented,

Even an old Boston pol said there was nothing wrong with black patronage...we did it, now maybe it's time for them to do it.

Other observers, however, saw this as a promotion of affirmative action. Joseph Delgardo, president of the Boston Educators Alliance of Massachusetts (BEAM) made sure his executive committee met often with Spillane in his first year: "We were getting in our shots, before he got to know the system...it's a strategy all people use, lay out their agendas...We were concerned he'd abide by the court order...and that he wouldn't downgrade the Affirmative Action Office, so we kept in touch and monitored that." An offshoot of BEAM, the Concerned Black Educators of Boston (CBEB), monitored affirmative action at the teacher level and pressed for a 25 percent black teaching staff. CBEB became the nucleus for a coalition of nearly 1,000 black teachers by the time Spillane took over.

The court spawned a "politics of desegregation." It created a black leadership that drew strength from a network that extended to the School Committee and the black and non-black minority community. A coalition was formed that Spillane had to address and his early appointments reflect this.

The fiscal problems Spillane faced when he took the job were unfairly laid at the doorstep of Robert Peterkin, a black. As the Deputy Superintendent for Management, he had control over the budget and personnel. In addition, Peterkin was a candidate for Spillane's job. Foresight tends to suggest that these conditions warranted a replacement for Peterkin. Indeed, as a school official said, Spillane could easily do this because "he had the votes on the committee."

However, Peterkin had close ties to the O'Bryant network and, in fact, was the highest ranking black official at school department headquarters and widely respected as an administrator. Even though Spillane had the votes to dismiss Peterkin, the signals Spillane got told him that "there was no way to move him out." Spillane had to decide if the issue warranted a school committee vote along racial lines.

Caught in this crossfire only two weeks into the job, Spillane decided to keep Peterkin. But Spillane used this situation to his advantage: "It was a good move," commented a school department employee, "Spillane kept saying that budget and personnel were all screwed up, but he could not and did not blame Peterkin for the mess." Spillane recounted,

> *I told him I was putting budget under a new deputy…He had to get out of that management and fiscal fiasco…it was beginning to reflect on him…and he wanted Operations and for me I wanted at least one black who was respected at central administration.*

This gave Spillane leverage to redirect two important bases of power (budget and personnel) to the Deputy Superintendent for Finance Administration, a person he selected, while at the same time keep Peterkin in a re-designed Deputy Superintendent for School Operations position.

Spillane also appointed a black woman as Personnel Director. The appointment came early in the first year which prompted one school official to say "It was a quick early black appointment...Spillane had to make some move to get credibility...it was good, she was working hand-in-glove with the black leadership."

Minority appointments were signals to a constituency and helped build leverage in the first year in much the same way that Spillane used signals and built leverage with the Mayor and business community when addressing the fiscal problems he inherited. But there were tradeoffs. A school department official summarized it this way:

> *Some of his (Spillane's) critics would say he kept some blacks in positions to keep the leadership happy...that's true and in light of what he said about accountability, it seems contradictory...but he had to keep people in some positions.*

Finally, the court, over the eight years of involvement in the Boston Public Schools, created sub-systems to protect judicial mandates that Spillane had to contend with.

The Department of Implementation is a good example. This department was established to monitor student assignments and transfers, transportation, public information and the overall desegregation of the system.[13]

The Department of Implementation, meant to be a tool for desegregation, became a source of political anxiety for Spillane. It clung to a student assignment process that more and more seemed illogical given demographic changes. So, "student assignment areas are the same today (1982) as in 1975...[despite] major shifts in population, major changes in neighborhood compositions and radical alterations in the composition of the student body."[14]

The Department of Implementation had the authority to take "specific measures" at certain schools whenever the ethnic composition of a district changed so that demographic forces did not result in a re-segregation of the public schools. The department could initiate changes in the "geocode units" in order to avoid "all black" and "all white" schools. But, the department refused to initiate any revision in the geocode maps.

Some observers estimated that from thirty to fifty percent of the schools were not in compliance with student desegregation standards established by the court. It struck Spillane squarely in the face when he visited one school.

> *When I walked into the Jeremiah Burke...I did not see a white young-ster in that school, and I went to every classroom. Didn't see one. I'm sure they were there and I'm sure I missed some, but it was obvious, it had to be 93 or 99 percent minority. Well, on paper, there were scores of white youngsters assigned to that school, but they never showed up...*[15]

The Department of Implementation seemed at the helm of control-ling the extent to which the schools could become further desegregated or segregated. It used its leverage to wring support from some School Committee members so Spillane could not impose his management authority in order to compete with demographic changes and revise the trend toward a re-segregation of the school system.

Another sub-system that the court created and that intervened in the management of Spillane's was the cadre of court-appointed experts and monitors. Court experts advised Judge Garrity on the prudence of school department initiatives and supervised compliance efforts. Court monitors were the "eyes and ears" of the court; they lodged themselves in key areas such as curriculum, staffing and resource management. They had over-sight responsibility for programs such as bi-lingual and special education. Monitors legitimized parent advocacy groups such as the state-created Bi-Lingual Masterpac and legitimized companion departments at school headquarters. The Special Education Unit, described to me as a "bureau-cracy unto itself" found support for their missionary zeal and relied on the court and its monitors to shield them from programs and budget cuts that Spillane made.

The often confusing array and presence of experts and monitors blurred the distinction between desegregation issues and educational issues. Spillane constantly found he needed to "protect his turf" as an educator and defend educational initiatives.

Spillane and School Committee President Jean McKeigue's propos-al for an experimental K–8 grade structure in one school district is an example. The proposal, used in other cities, set up a pilot school that was intended to eliminate the troubled middle schools as well as provide an opportunity for students to remain in the same school for a longer period. This would allow for some stability in their education. When Spillane and McKeigue presented the plan to Judge Garrity in April, he rejected it saying it might encourage feeder problems that had led to segregated high schools in the past.[16] Garrity's decision, however, was prompted by the findings of a court-appointed desegregation expert who found the experiment unsound for desegregation purposes because "it does not have clear, intended and planned consequences for furthering racial equity."[17] Only after increasing public commentary and media support claiming these educational initiatives did not threaten the court order did Garrity change his mind and give his approval of the plan.

Not only do issues become blurred by the presence of court experts and monitors but so does management. Court representatives were known to give covert direction to both senior officials and middle management staff. The practice was not uncommon in the past, as one former superintendent found: "Court experts gave oral instructions to key senior officials, who understandably were uncertain as to whether they worked for the experts, the court, or the superintendent."[18]

An equally restrictive sub-system Spillane had to contend with was the formal court hearing. This was the basis of all communication between the court and the school department. In fact, he did not meet with Judge Garrity until December and then only to present a review of his initiatives and plans for the school system. He made his presentation from the "witness chair" in the courtroom.

Spillane found the formal court hearing and the inability to talk informally with the court abridged his efforts to manage the school system. The restrictive communication style of the court was an embarrassment. One parent leader commented: "I think this was important...every time the superintendent or School Committee goes to court, it's a formal hearing...that's a very difficult way to communicate and this affected Spillane's vision of power." Even a lawyer assigned to the court admitted that "I guess it's his (Garrity's) judicial style...he works through attorneys…he doesn't encourage conferences in chambers while others may do so."

Spillane's Response: The Gloves Are Off

Spillane turned to the media in order to focus the court's intrusions into the management of the school system. It was a way to compete with each of the sub-systems as well as compensate for the authority the court gave to external and internal constituencies using a unified strategy. "He took on the court" as a source of authority. It was a risky strategy, commented one school official, because "The general theory around here was that you don't fool with the Judge; that gets him madder and he can hit you harder."

Spillane initiated this strategy quite by accident although he knew he had to do it at some point. While at a conference in up-state New York, Spillane was called by a reporter from the *Boston Herald American.* Only two months into his first year, the reporter was interested in how he felt about his new job. During the course of the conversation, the discussion drifted to the court's efforts to desegregate the schools. He responded by saying that busing had not produced the desired results of a quality desegregated education in Boston and noted that the "track record for busing has been dismal."

The headline in the *Boston Herald American* the next day featured "Spillane: Busing Failed."[19] The remark opened the floodgate of controversy and sparked a continual sequel in the newspapers about the merits of busing. The remark was seen as an assault on the Federal court order generally and Judge Garrity in particular. "The Judge," commented one court advisor "was seen as positive force and voice in desegregation…those who historically opposed [him] were seen as opponents to desegregation and minority rights…but also not a friend of the court."

The ripples invited comments by both the court and the School Committee. The court defended busing saying "There is no other way to maintain a desegregated system in Boston except to bus students" while School Committee President McKeigue countered that "If you look at the schools, you'll see we're busing all black kids to all black schools in white neighborhoods...[and that while federal control has achieved] a certain goal...it's now time for the court to get out of the schools."[20]

The irony of this accidental strategy is that the issue was on people's minds but no one at the school department made any attempt to bring it out in the open. One school observer noted that "Sure, everyone knew busing was a problem; he (Spillane) realized that and that there was great polarization on that issue...it was an absolute block to developing quality education. But no one said anything. If you were on one side you were a racist and bigot...but if on the other side, you were interested only in forced busing."

Spillane admitted the strategy may have been a bit off: "I knew I put my foot in my mouth...what I really wanted to say was look at what's at the end of the bus ride. But I was the first one in Boston to say it...no one believed I said it or would say it. Yeah, I know it was interpreted as a racist statement but I knew I needed to kick it (the issue) off the dime sometime...so it was then not later but if I was wrong then everyone would come out against it; as it was, everyone knew it was true." When I pressed the issue in an interview concerning whether he thought it was a good strategy, Spillane conceded,

> Yeah...you don't say things like that...but it was important sometime to serve notice on the Judge...to tell the Judge that he didn't have a patsy here.

Once it happened, it was important for him "to shore it up quickly." For this, he relied on a growing constituency that supported his efforts to bring financial control and management authority to the school system. Spillane recounted, he "followed it up in several interviews in several papers why busing failed...to tell people what's at the end of the bus ride. It wasn't really quality education but rather that the system had equal opportunity for a terrible education not a quality education."

But beyond that, commented Katherine Kelley, Spillane's attack on Garrity did not backfire because he "appointed black educators to important positions at the school department. This gave him support in the black community...he was able to ameliorate the issue with Garrity."

Spillane knew there was support for his position even in the black community. A parent leader analyzed the issue this way:

> *...he had gained a sense that there was positive support. I think he figured it out and played to it...busing was unpopular and the desegregation plan had lost favor even among its proponents...the plan just did not work.*

Spillane pressed his case in the media for how the court intruded in the management of the school system. He pointed to the Department of Implementation and the court monitors and experts as examples of this intrusion. He accused the Judge in an impromptu speech before 500 dinner guests at the annual banquet of the Greater Boston Chamber of Commerce of trying to manage the city school system from the bench and said,

> *We cannot continue to have this system managed by [experts] and monitors who meet twice a month...The intrusions are inhibiting better ways to desegregate the district and improve programs.*[21]

Spillane relied on this support and the media to keep up a dialogue with Judge Garrity. This was significant since the court had set in motion a negotiations process that brought together plaintiffs and defendants.

Spillane could not effectively breach this process (and the court's power) without developing his own power base. Thus, he turned to other constituencies and, in doing so, he promoted a public support for the schools.

Chapter 7
Public Support

Just prior to his taking office, Spillane amplified on the importance of public support.

As the educational leader of the school system…I think that's (public support) absolutely critical. If they (the public) can have confidence in me, they'll have confidence in my ability to run the school system.[1]

Spillane did not say "client" support. This was one of the first choices he made after he became superintendent. He conceded that his strategy involved a choice. He noted, "only 10% of the city has kids in school. So that means most don't have them in school…The constituency has to be the Mayor, business community and organizations."

The schools "just didn't have a significant political base from which to draw." Rather, it was certain individuals and groups that had a political base. Even the taxpayers themselves stood as an attractive element of support because

Parent groups were in terrible disarray…plus just by their membership they don't count. But I can tell you who counts; like when police and fire stations were closing, people really demonstrated. I mean huge demonstrations. But when the schools closed, there wasn't a whimper…just no grass roots energy. Those that protested loss of police and fire services, they're the guts of the city.

The city population stood in stark contrast to the school's parent population. The city's population reflected a 70 percent white and 30 percent black and other minority population while the schools reversed this ratio.

This contrast produced a void. It left the schools without a viable constituency. It left the schools without protection from prying hands. Spillane found a number of different attempts were being made to take control of the schools and "get a piece of the action." The court threatened the schools with receivership; the Mayor proposed legislation that would put the schools under one individual who reported directly to him; a Boston University official proposed that he run the schools as a private independent contractor; and the Boston Teachers Union spoke of negotiating curriculum rights.

It was left to Spillane to fill this void.

Power Brokers

One group was the Mayor-business community-taxpayers. They controlled the three essential ingredients of power in Boston: votes, jobs, and money. Votes gave the four-term Mayor a strong political position in the city. In a direct way, his constituency elected him; but his attitude toward the schools could in turn influence his constituency's image of the schools. When he abandoned the schools, so did his constituency; when he smiled at the schools, his constituency looked more kindly on them. Jobs were equally the province of the Mayor and the business community. Both had the influence to open a market of career opportunities for Boston graduates. And, money was critical to the schools. The Mayor provided supplemental budgets while the business community supported diverse projects.

Spillane recognized this and in his first speech to the administrative staff three weeks into the job, he stressed that in addition to instruction and accountability, a co-equal priority was

[establishing] our financial and managerial credibility with the Mayor, the business community and the citizens of Boston.[2]

Mayor White

White's embrace can be life-giving to an institution like the schools that desperately need both the funds and the civic interest [he] is capable of stimulating.[3] Spillane's strategy for approaching Mayor White was simple.

Here's the key. The Mayor loves me. I'm the first superintendent that stood as a lightning rod for the schools. I said, "I'll take the heat (not like we do so much in education)..." I've been to meetings where I said publicly that we can't blame the Mayor, we can't blame the government for lack of funds, we can't blame the parents, we can't blame the school committee...the fact that 30% of our high school students can't read is not anyone else's fault. We've got to straighten out our own house then we can go after the Mayor for [more money].

He told me there weren't many options. "How in the hell could we not let the teachers go when the city was in an economic free fall and city workers went without pay for a couple of weeks."

This helped to establish his credibility with the Mayor. It served to place Spillane near the network of power brokers. The Mayor influenced an important ingredient in Spillane's effort to manage the environment—civic interest. Spillane could appeal to the civic interest—community taxpayers—through the Mayor and even build support for himself in the process.

Mayor White is regarded as a political institution in Boston. He was thought to be an autocrat by some but revered by others for bringing city government closer to the people by establishing "Little City Halls" throughout the city. He could make tough decisions by closing fire stations when the city faced budget issues and many believed he could do so with the schools. He built a political machine so that many people compared him to Mayor (Chicago) Daley. His political esteem was important to Spillane. However, the problems at the school department kept White aloof and distant from the schools. The schools were politically expedient. The image needed to be changed. A prominent reporter noted that Spillane used the media for

...building a perception, like he never challenged the Mayor but instead he was impressing the Mayor with managerial abilities and not taking on the Mayor with a fight...that was important.

Business Community

Spillane spent his first two months developing important linkages with the business community. This included meeting with two influential groups: The Trilateral Council for Quality Education and the Coordinating Council (The Vault). Both groups represented the "vested interests of business in the city" and played an important role in Spillane's quest for a political base. The Trilateral Council had a school orientation and provided resources for the schools. On the other hand, the Coordinating Committee, whose membership comprised the chief executive officers of the 20 largest companies in the city, provided an on-going mechanism for dialogue and issue discussion. It was an assemblage of Yankee corporate leadership designed to strengthen Boston's economic underpinnings.

These groups were important to Spillane. One observer commented,

Spillane needed this commitment...they were important because the schools didn't have any credibility. The business community gave credibility to the schools...I guess it was a case of "position politics."

In Boston, it was common "to talk in terms of populist attitudes or position politics. To make the business community, downtown business, look bad...it was a useful political position because the business community was looked on as rich suburbanites." Spillane did not take his lead from this history but from what he saw emerging as a new and important focus in Boston politics. He took his lead from Mayor White who was saying that the growth of business in downtown Boston could provide important taxes to ease the city's financial problems. "The downtown business," White preached, "should not be seen as an ogre...the strength of [this city's] neighborhoods live in those towers (downtown offices)."[4]

Spillane met with many people in the Trilateral Council both individually and at meetings. "He listened to them and their problems early out, like the school management issues and how to get at them...but he emphasized he wanted a strong cooperative relationship. He made that particularly clear." He met with the Coordinating Committee and developed a close working relationship with its executive secretary who "became involved in the day-to-day events in Spillane's first few months." This gave him an important advantage, even a window on the city and the political infrastructure. Spillane's calendar reveals he kept up this relationship, as well as many others, through frequent private meetings, lunches and dinners.

Close ties with the business community also included a working relationship with the Boston Municipal Research Bureau and its associate executive director. The BMRB, a privately financed research organization, became an important asset to Spillane as he went about reorganizing the finance and management areas of the school department. They had been in constant contact with the school department and knew the personnel involved with the budget problems. The BMRB made some important suggestions for reorganization and were especially helpful to Spillane in choosing some key personnel so he could avoid a "mass firing" strategy which could have caused serious morale problems within the school department.

Two other network linkages were with the Boston Finance Commission (Fin Com) and the Corporation for Boston (CFB). The Boston Finance Commission is a State agency created to oversee the city of Boston's spending. While it had little to do with education, it made policy recommendations that affected the management of the schools—i.e., Tregor Bill. The Corporation for Boston, only a year old when Spillane took over, is a private "city-wide leadership organization whose prime mission is to enhance communication among various sectors of the city and to intervene quietly [in order] to combat the consequences of racism."[5] Both groups helped Spillane deflect some of the mounting criticism that confronted him because of his stance on busing and violence; issues that raised the spectra of Spillane's racial insensitivity and threatened his chances for a four-year contract. It was the CFB who worked to patch up the growing gulf between Spillane and the black School Committee members.

The Universities

The court established a program that "paired" universities and colleges, businesses and cultural institutions with the Boston Public Schools. The purpose of the program was to mobilize specific resources in the city to bring about systematic changes and encourage program initiatives. Universities and colleges were specially singled-out by the court "to support, assist, and participate in the development of educational excellence within and among the public schools of Boston."[6]

The program paired some 25 universities and colleges with the Boston Public Schools. A (University) President's Steering Committee monitored the involvement of the universities. The program, however, met with only minimal success. One member of the Trilateral Council (which served like the President's Steering Committee and coordinated the pairings between businesses and the schools) noted, "Even though there were some successes like starting a newspaper, getting outside speakers and developing career opportunity programs, the general attitude among the headmasters was that they were not interested. It was awfully low on their priority list." A former Boston superintendent added,

> ...academic reactions ranged from enthusiastic to grudging compliance. Sometimes the [school] and college so joined together simply did not fit...[And] the academic community squabbled increasingly about central staff support.[7]

"As a result," commented one university official, "after eight years of the pairings, it was difficult to find any real change, lasting change."

Spillane gave the program greater visibility and attention within his administration. He assigned a top assistant to work closely with the President's Steering Committee. He pushed the issue in his accountability program; the success of the pairings became a criterion in the evaluation of school administrators. This effort brought him closer to the university establishment and its key actors.

Taxpayers

Mayor White was a key to Spillane's initiatives to gather support from the taxpayers. Spillane rarely gave a speech where he did not mention this important constituency. He attracted their attention by his efforts to install accountability measures so that they could "get their money's worth." His strong adherence to a suspension policy to curb violence in the schools stood him in good stead with the taxpayers who saw the schools as a "blackboard jungle." This was a tradeoff; it created a veneer of racism over his administration since suspensions for black students were more than twice as high as those for white students.

Spillane relied on both his association with Mayor White and his use of the media to convey his sentiments to the taxpayers. He hoped to restore the confidence of the predominantly white population of the city.

Those I interviewed felt that the overtures to these power brokers helped Spillane "build a guard...all these people were a shield around the schools. They gave the schools a measure of protection by having this constituency." These initiatives also protected Spillane and "created a wall of power for him."

New Voices

Another group that influenced Spillane's attempt to manage the environment was the various parent organizations. I refer to them as parent advocacy groups because they pressed for the concerns of parents and focused their energy around the needs and interests of the "clients of the school system." While power brokers wanted to influence the decision making authority in the school system, parent advocacy groups wanted to share decision making authority. The Citywide Parents Advisory Council (CPAC) was an influential parent advisory group Spillane dealt with in his first year.

A month on the job, Spillane recommended that the school committee cut CPAC's budget from $700,000 to $400,000. In light of the substantial cuts he was making in school programs, the reduction seemed fair. CPAC did not think so and an argument ensued.

Two weeks later the argument became public. In a press conference, CPAC criticized Spillane for his "downplaying" the Federal court requirement that the school department fund the parent council and pay its staff. CPAC used this opportunity to attack Spillane's moves to cut programs that affected minority students (i.e., kindergarten) as well as his failure to redress a "chaotic opening of school." One parent leader argued: "We believe there is little education currently taking place in the Boston Public Schools." Another was more direct: "I just don't see any progress. He's been in the superintendent's seat for two months now...I would mark his first Boston report card with an F."[8]

I was curious about why Spillane would venture into such a confrontation so early in his term especially over such a small amount of money. So I asked a number of individuals about these early developments. The answers clearly reflect a strategy for dealing with parent advocacy groups. One CPAC leader noted,

> *He made choices...choices were important to him in the first year. I think he said he could get parents by winning them over then delivering the services to prove it or the hell with winning them over, I'll do that if I deliver the product, the services. Yeah, that was the choice and, I guess, it makes sense.*

And the leader of an influential community-based organization added that "it was a very political decision he made, not going after parents, not courting parents...or community-based organizations."

Spillane's own response was direct. "They are paid, professional parents. I think that creates adversarial relations. They consider themselves monitors for the court...they should support the administration's goals."[9]

His strategy was, then, to "deliver the product"; he used this as a way to gain the support of a wider audience as well as promote an image that his administrative priorities reflected professional goals.

There were reasons why he could choose this strategy. For one thing, parent advocacy groups had different goals and generally did not support each other. CPAC's quest for authority as the legitimate parent group put them in competition with older more established parent constituencies in Boston like the Home-School Association (HSA). For more than 70 years, this association served neighborhood schools and gave parents an opportunity to exercise some influence over their child's education. HSA, with a predominantly white membership, objected to these "new upstarts" and felt a threat of disestablishment. One HSA parent leader commented,

> *They were set up by the court and were new to the scene...they pushed for their own goals like forced busing...They were written up in the*

newspapers...I think you just lose sight of what schools are supposed to do.

CPAC argued with the influential Citywide Education Coalition (CWEC) over the CWEC's image as a parent group. CWEC's publicity flier notes that it is a ten-year old educational reform organization that focuses attention on citizen involvement. It does this through forums and workshops as well as widely circulated publications about educational issues. In past years, the flier used the word "parent" not citizen. An official of CWEC made it clear to me that I should be sure to say they represented citizens, not parents, because

> *That's CPAC's political interest...when we used to be thought of as a parent group, CPAC felt threatened. They felt that with the court order and funds they were the legitimate parent group in the city and objected to us calling ourselves a parent group.*

Within the confines of the external environment, interest groups competed for authority and access to the schools and school district polity making.

Another reason why Spillane could choose this strategy comes from the racial discord evident among parent groups. While some parent leaders served as officers in both CWEC and CPAC, differences about desegregation efforts precluded a united front. Even the minority-oriented CPAC was threatened by racial discord. One observer suggested that CPAC was "divided by racism...divided by blacks and whites. They (court) wanted one black and one white to lead but that fell apart."

This divisiveness filtered down into the district and school site bi-racial parent councils. One court advisor reflected: "[The court] strongly supported these bi-racial councils. It felt that these councils, with blacks and whites, should encourage parents to talk together, especially about their children. But different views about the purpose of desegregation persisted and fueled the divisiveness that was played out in program cuts." One observer noted, these bi-racial councils were "side stages where all the issues Spillane dealt with could be played out...So you can't just say that the community is one large stage but it has lots of smaller stages." It was these smaller stages that magnified the racial issues Spillane faced in his first year.

Spillane thought that CPAC (and other parent advocacy groups like the Bi-Lingual Masterpac and the Hispanic El Comite) had questionable motives. Spillane noted, and others I spoke with agreed,

> *The CPAC...They're like the teachers union...[They are really saying] "Parents you stay out. We'll represent you." I don't get letters from them (CPAC). I get letters from their lawyers...That's really a disaster. Those are the kind of people that politically are looking for their own political gain (and) deliberately try to put a wedge between the superintendent and the school committee.*[10]

Parents advocacy groups wanted a share of the decision making authority that rested with Spillane. The court legitimized their efforts by making CPAC participants in the selection and evaluation of personnel. Perhaps this explains why Spillane found (nor did he try to change) a negative attitude toward parent advocacy groups when he came. One school observer close to Spillane noted,

> *I think it happened this way. Spillane goes into this advisors and says, "Look I've got to speak to these people, who are they? What do I say?" So they answer, "Oh yeah, those people, they have a half million dollar budget and they haven't done a damn thing." So he goes out and tells them things like that.*

Spillane was able to read this environment and, as a result, know what the consequences would be from a confrontation with CPAC. One parent guessed,

> *I don't think he prejudged the situation but he heard the static. Parent groups in Boston are a mess and they were. He took one look at the source of power of the parent groups and found it was the Judge and he was disgusted. He doesn't like fetters in his power.*

Spillane built his agenda accordingly. He chose to build his own power base and credibility in order to define priorities. His relationship with Mayor White and the business community reflects his agenda (and choice). In addition, he also built some bridges with the leadership of HSA and CWEC.

Both HSA and CWEC were divested of their earlier authority as a result of the court order installing CPAC as the representative parent group. And, both the Mayor and the business community were also on "the outs." What Spillane did was to turn to those individuals and organizations who were on the margin of school district policy making to build a power base. These individuals and organizations each had a constituency. Spillane could rely on this to develop a power base. A network existed among these four "latent" sources of power (Mayor, business community, HSA and CWEC). Indeed, CWEC officers served on the board of the influential Corporation for Boston and the predominantly white HSA and CWEC could supply attractive support for Mayor White and Spillane.

These relationships influenced Spillane. At the urging of the leaders of CWEC, Spillane held monthly meetings with the leadership of the parent advocacy groups (including CPAC) and visited each of the nine school districts to meet with parents. One parent leader commented, "I told him to go out to the districts and don't wait to get invited. Meet the parents and hear their concerns. He said OK and did it. He seemed willing to make the right moves."

Both efforts got poor reviews. One parent remarked "Maybe it wasn't such a good idea. Lots of people came. They were glad that he did that since superintendents in Boston don't do that. But the parents were frustrated. They wanted answers; why so many program cuts? They didn't want to hear his problems. They wanted a plan of action and he couldn't give them one."

The monthly meetings fell apart after three months for the same reasons. One CPAC leader left abruptly after one meeting saying "I'm not coming again. It's a waste of my time…all he's going to do is defend himself."

What came across was that Spillane was unwilling to compromise his fiscal priorities for educational priorities. He was seen as aloof. A CWEC official noted,

It's just the type of superintendent he is. I think he believed it was nice

to have parents around…but I got the impression that he was saying "I'm the guy who's got to make it work. I have to use my energies and expend them on the staff. If I can make that work, all the parents will be behind me. I've got to do that…then others will back me."

Spillane's preference was the management of the school system. "As far as things were concerned," commented one businessman, "management was what was needed. If you say educational leader, that doesn't fly. It was management…if he hadn't taken hold of that he would never have been re-appointed." Another observer was equally direct:

Talk about style…if you're thinking about philosophy of education, Bud Spillane is not the one who comes to mind. But if you want to talk about how to manage a large, complex school system, then you'd think of Bud Spillane.

Parent advocacy groups expected a more sensitive style of communication. Spillane was direct, even, at times, offensive. One black leader made this observation:

When he met with black folks, he was not uncomfortable, not nervous; if anything, he was inappropriately comfortable. He came across as arrogant…he spoke as though he was inside them not outside them.

Others criticized Spillane for "listening to give an impression rather than listening to gain an impression."

They also expected an "image of fairness." This was due, in part, to different interests competing for scarce resources in a system plagued by mismanagement. "The easiest thing he could have done," noted a Bi-Lingual Masterpac official, "was to get them all together and say let's work together and find out what to do. To educate them all to the dilemmas and start balancing rights and needs so that no one felt ignored. At least appear to make the process look fair. He would have found us a piece of cake." On more than one occasion, I heard people say concerning his approach to CPAC that

he could have taken a different tact…he could have said, "I want to work with you. I see you have a budget but I don't see what you've done. From now on, I'll be involved. I'll give you a year; keep the dollars but I want to see results and these are the kind of results I want to see."

Spillane's failure to respond to these leadership needs taken together with his attitude toward CPAC and other advocacy brokers affected his relationship with minorities. He lost substantial support from key minority elements in the city. Indeed, CPAC intensified their criticism of Spillane. With linkages to black School Committee members, they nearly forced a vote for a four-year contract based on racial lines. Spillane wanted to avoid a racial vote.

Chapter 8
The Contract Fight

The value of stability to children, parents and staff cannot be overstated. Associated with this issue of stability is the Superintendency. As soon as possible, it is critical that this School Committee know who will be providing the administrative leadership over the next four years. I will ask the Committee to establish a process to determine, by February 22, whether Dr. Spillane will be offered a full, four-year contract...[1]

At a School Committee meeting on January 25, two weeks after her inaugural address, McKeigue suggested a list of criteria to evaluate Spillane. She told the Committee she wanted an objective evaluation; the School Committee could review the list and suggest modifications. She promised public discussions on the evaluation. In an interview just prior to the meeting, she suggested her support for Spillane.

One of the first charges given Superintendent Spillane was to get the financial and management picture into shape. I think he has done that. We know how many people we employ, we know at what level we're spending...He has also addressed the matter of curriculum...He's only been here now for five months, and I think he's done an amazing job.[2]

McKeigue's comments were followed almost immediately by the concerns of O'Bryant and McGuire, the two black members on the School Committee. It gave the contract vote new significance. In an interview with *The Boston Globe*, both members voiced their concern over Spillane's racial insensitivity since becoming superintendent. While admitting "there hasn't been much of a track record because he hasn't been here that long,"[3] they raised the following points.

Spillane's strong position on violence was viewed as being aimed at black students. In the black community, school violence was seen as a racial code word.

Spillane's comment that "busing failed" left the impression he was against desegregation and supported anti-busing advocates.

Spillane's decision to place a white staff member in charge of re-writing the curriculum was an embarrassment to the black administrator who prepared the original draft. His subsequent push to dismiss the administrator prompted O'Bryant to say "I haven't seen any other senior official get the kind of abuse or lack of professional courtesy that [she] has."[4]

Spillane's decision to have the Office of Equal Opportunity report directly to the Deputy Superintendent for Finance (also in charge of personnel) raised questions about his commitment to affirmative action.

Some of the criticisms were not new. In a memo to Spillane the previous November, O'Bryant criticized him for his handling of the curriculum incident. O'Bryant also said that he had overstepped his authority by making public statements on policy questions. O'Bryant said Spillane had no authority to warn teachers they would be fired if they went out on strike, nor did he have the authority to question the success (or failure) of the court-ordered desegregation plan.

Spillane admitted he meant to say he would recommend the dismissal of striking teachers, a power reserved to the School Committee but defended his statement on busing saying it was taken out of context. An analysis of this background suggests the flap with O'Bryant in November was a prelude to the contract vote. By that time, O'Bryant, and later McGuire, were getting strong signals from their constituencies about Spillane's questionable appearance concerning racial issues.

Political imagery and behind the scenes escapades surrounded Spillane's bid for a contract. He was an attractive candidate for some, a questionable and even unacceptable candidate for others. At their meeting on February 8, the School Committee heard O'Bryant and McGuire request a delay in the February 22 contract vote to allow for a further review of Spillane's sensitivity to racial issues. They were joined by a four-member delegation of black and Hispanic leaders and a black State Representative, Melvin H. King, who were even more specific. They wanted the Committee to postpone the vote and seek other candidates for the superintendency. The School Committee voted 3–2, along racial lines, to deny the request by O'Bryant and McGuire. The fall-out from that vote prompted one school official to say that "all hell broke loose in the next ten days."

O'Bryant called the vote a "racist decision"[5] and left the meeting abruptly saying "That exercise shows it is business as usual on issues affecting black people and people of color. As long as we have a committee that brushes us aside...It's a sad day."[6] Both O'Bryant and McGuire attested they wanted more time to gather information so that they were certain Spillane was "a pro-integration Superintendent who is clear as a bell on what he does."[7] Representative King was more outspoken. After the meeting, he called at the white school committee members and warned "We are not going to let you get away with this...He [Spillane] doesn't have the support of the minority community."[8]

The meeting evidenced an emotional and heated exchange between white and black school committee members. McCluskey rebuffed O'Bryant saying the issue wasn't really race but O'Bryant's concern over the way Spillane handled the curriculum incident. McCluskey commented, "The catalyst here is that the sacred ground of a senior officer [Miller] was trod upon."[9] Spillane, after the meeting, remarked that O'Bryant and McGuire's claims of racial insensitivity were "greatly unfounded and shallow accusations."[10] He added, that the issue (race) was a smokescreen for O'Bryant and McGuire's desire for political patronage in the school system.

While O'Bryant denied the charges, it did not prevent the media from promoting that image. *The Boston Globe* reported,

> *O'Bryant and McGuire appear to be concerned with protecting the jobs*

of black administrators, who have been present in the central office for only a few years. Skeptics view their concern as an echo of the traditional system of patronage in the Boston schools… [11]

Still, O'Bryant and McGuire, with support from the minority community, pressed their case in the media and kept race an important issue in the evaluation process. There were important reasons for them to do so. If Spillane won a four-year contract, he would oversee the school's role in negotiations currently underway to have the Federal court withdraw from the Boston School Desegregation Plan. For blacks, it was important to have someone at the helm who could press for the rights of blacks and other minorities. They also knew that black influence at the School Committee was expected to erode under the city's new redistricting plan that would enlarge the School Committee to thirteen members in 1984. (Under this plan, the School Committee would seat four members elected at-large and nine members elected from the districts; all current school committee members were elected at-large.) A number of school observers thought redistricting was especially important for O'Bryant and McGuire. One commented,

Well…the blacks saw it was their own system with 70% of the schools being black (and non-black minorities)…they probably thought that they had to make some gains now before redistricting because it was generally true that the most they could get under the new plan was four votes.

For others, though, there was another important issue associated with the contract vote. White school committee members felt a great urgency to settle the contract mattered as a result of the instability brought on by having three superintendents in 14 months. They tried to re-focus the contract vote in terms of this instability. So did the media. One news editor noted,

If we didn't have this instability with so many superintendents then Spillane might have had some real problems. Even though it (contract vote) centered around racism, most whites and some blacks didn't think so…They didn't come away with the idea that he was a racist. He was

doing OK so they (minority community) didn't have that ultimate card that he screwed up so badly that they had to get rid of him...There was no malfeasance and he did some good things. But the real issue was the history...so much instability.

These issues surfaced from the February 8 meeting and focused the rhetoric that appeared almost daily in the media. It also focused attention, once again, on O'Bryant and Spillane. One black school observer close to Spillane commented,

Look, you can tell things to Spillane in private and disagree with him and that's OK...but when it hits the public, I mean, he's concerned about that image. He wants to do something.

He continued,

And, O'Bryant...I mean to the black community he's the Black Superintendent...he had to look good too...minorities see O'Bryant and know the School Committee always had the power, superintendent was their director, they told him what to do...people saw O'Bryant and said "at last we've arrived."

Spillane left the February 8 meeting saying to a reporter: "I interpret this [vote] as a four-year contract."[12] The media was less certain, somewhat critical but supportive of a four-year contract. One editorial noted that Spillane

can be abrasive, impatient and even rude...but the attempt to brand him a racist...strikes us as a bad case of overkill.[13]

Referring to the curriculum incident, the editorial noted "it could have been avoided with just a little more courtesy on Spillane's part [but] he is guilty of rudeness more than racism."[14]

Still another editorial, entitled "Blacks and Spillane," questioned the charge of racism and asked: "Where is the evidence?"[15] Furthermore, while questioning Spillane's tact for his comments about busing, it added "But is there anyone, of any race, interested in urban education, who hasn't wondered about the efficacy of busing."[16] "If anything," it continued,

Spillane has been insensitive not to race but to the sensitivity of racial issues in Boston. That was a mistake; but one that can be rectified if given the opportunity. His black critics should back off and give him that opportunity.[17]

Spillane made some conscious choices during his first five months in order to build support for his contract. He focused his attention on the Mayor and the business community as well as university officials. Each had an important role in helping Spillane establish credibility for the school system and build public support for the schools. These were the power brokers Spillane felt he needed to influence in order to build his own power base. The strategy seemed to work; one school committee member told him in December: "You know, you sonofabitch, we couldn't get rid of you if we wanted to."

Spillane attributed this support to building credibility and noted, "Credibility starts the day you start...it starts building from the first day. It had to for me because I only had an eleven-month contract."

Spillane's efforts to establish credibility were tied directly to signals he sent to the constituency he wanted to support him. His effort to stay within a $210 million budget and avoid, at all costs, a deficit were signals to the Mayor and the business community. It was clear that he needed to convince the taxpayers that spending was under control and that financial records were available and accurate. Even by mid-September, after six weeks on the job, the School Committee began advertising that finances were under control (even though it would take another three months to prove it). He noted,

Building credibility is difficult at best. It means you've got to go talk to parents, civic leaders, business groups, service organizations...I was giving, at times, two speeches a week...like when I went to the Rotary Club or somewhere else, it's just making enough sense to them so that they can trust me and at the same time come to understand the schools.

Spillane built enough credibility so he got the support from the Mayor and business community. Perhaps sensing the pressure that was building over his contract vote, this support moved for a public announcement indicating a vote of confidence. He got it just before Christmas when the City Council voted him a $10,000 raise for the following year. "I was lobbied for his raise," commented one city councilor, "and I know others were lobbied also. It wasn't high on our priority list but I'm sure when Spillane talked with Mayor White, the Mayor said 'Don't worry, I'll get what you want in the end.'"

Still Spillane had to contend with the minority community. One parent organization leader suggested that Spillane was his own worst enemy.

There were lots of meetings going on in the fall, meetings in the minority community. I went to them because of my position and saw what went on...people saying the guy is a racist. Who couldn't believe it since he was so combative. You can't deal that way...There are different ground rules here. I don't know if he's arrogant or just stupid. If he used his head he could have gotten all he wanted with less arrogance and more modesty.

The day after the February 8 vote, Spillane, before television cameras and the press, met with the Search Committee that interviewed him for the job. The meeting was called by President McKeigue so that the Committee could offer their views on his performance. Before the Committee, which included parent, neighborhood and business representatives, Spillane addressed the issue of his racial sensitivity and stressed his minority appointments. He commented,

I go by my track record...In the areas of insensitivity, I manage a large, complex operation that frankly needed strong management...I think I have been extremely sensitive in every opportunity where I could have been insensitive.[18]

Limited to four minutes, each speaker offered their views about Spillane's performance according to a list prepared by McKeigue. Spillane's supporters pointed out his achievements in finance and curriculum. But it was not until the television cameras left that Spillane's most vocal critics had a chance to question Spillane and raise their concerns about racial insensitivity. Many doubted the usefulness of the meeting and criticized it as a "bogus process" which promoted a "circus atmos-

phere" by the presence of TV crews. One black leader was equally direct
and said that "he and others were railroaded."

Several civic groups alarmed at the growing hostility that surrounded
the contract vote requested to intervene. The most influential of these
was the Corporation for Boston (CFB), a private multi-racial public service organization of business, university and community leaders. Acting in
key roles were Hubie Jones, CFB President, and Hassan Minor, Jr., CFB
Director. At the time, Jones noted,

> *Our concern was to get off the confrontation, polarization course...What
> we were most concerned about was...for the School Committee to begin
> to work together with each other in a different way...Because unless the
> Superintendent has [their] support, he can't move the system.*[19]

Minor noted another significant reason for a compromise: "It was
important that the [white] members of the School Committee understand
how the [contract] vote was being perceived in the minority community."[20] If the vote was divided along racial lines, the minority community
would have thought Spillane was not concerned with educating their children.[21]

The CFB met daily with the principal characters in the contract vote
and held many hours of private meetings during the week following the
February 8 vote. They arranged for Spillane to meet privately with
O'Bryant and McGuire. One week later, on February 17, at a news conference sponsored by the CFB, the School Committee and Spillane
announced they had reached a compromise: Spillane agreed to delay the
contract vote to March 3 and agreed to give a "major speech" on March
2 addressing the question of his racial insensitivity. School observers told
me that the agreement was predicated on Spillane getting a unanimous
vote.

Spillane also took under advisement "some personnel suggestions"
made by the CFB. These suggestions involved the appointment and reassignment of black administrators as well as white administrators. But
Jones was quick to point out that the suggestions did not entail political
patronage because they were made by the multi-racial leadership of
CFB.[22]

The peace effort was scored by the media as a major achievement. After the meeting, O'Bryant noted, "It's clear to me now that there is better understanding on both sides on what is necessary to make the system work."[23] While uncommitted about how he would vote, he added, "From the positive spirit expressed here today, I think we will be able to work out our differences."[24] McGuire was less optimistic and noted "Peace doesn't mean all the issues have been resolved."[25]

These comments give the contract vote another dimension. The fight for a contract was also a fight over management rights and administrative authority. It was, commented a CFB official, a move (along with other moves) "for Spillane to get control of the School Committee." Minor noted that the thinking in the city was the School Committee was the power and the superintendent its director, doing what he or she is told. Spillane, school observers felt, recognized this and pushed for control over the School Committee. One noted, "Like the layoffs, the contract vote had a psychological impact on the School Committee. They were not prepared for all that was happening, and some of them were damaged personally." Indeed, Spillane was advised when he came

> *[That he wouldn't] survive if he compromises with [them]...He must move with bold strokes before they [School Committee] have time to stop him.*[26]

But the issue of administrative authority became clouded by racial overtones. O'Bryant and McGuire, observers told me, worked hard to build a constituency and get elected to the School Committee where they could establish a base of power and exert influence. They were unlikely to concede that effort and power to Spillane who they could not trust to oversee their own legitimate priorities.

Spillane also met privately with his own supporters and key community leaders following the February 17 news conference. One business executive noted,

> *He got a lot of outside support because we realized he was one of the best we had...while not perfect, we all thought, let's try to keep him, but get him to realize he had to stay especially with the lack of stability in the*

system…it was just too chaotic not to get re-appointed. We just had to make it known that there were just a lot of reasons why he should get re-appointed.

In written evaluations requested by McKeigue in a letter she sent to parent, business and community organizations, Spillane received high marks for his work in budget and curriculum as well as his efforts to bring strong management to the school department. Among the evaluations, Mayor White endorsed Spillane saying, "In my opinion, his performance has been superb."[27] Seventeen college presidents also endorsed Spillane and praised him for improving relationships between the school department and the university "pairing" system.

Spillane did not receive an endorsement from minority parent groups and black leadership organizations. Minority community leaders kept up the assault and pressed their concerns. Led by Rep. Mel King, they criticized the CFB negotiated peace settlement. They noted they had little input in the process and that at least one CFB leader, who housed Spillane for a period of time after he was hired, was not neutral on the subject of the vote.

Both the meetings with his supporters and the evaluation letters underscored the necessity for Spillane to get a positive vote on his contract that did not reflect the racial issue. One school observer commented,

Look…he knew he had two votes, maybe three. But the negotiations proved to him he would look bad, like a racial appointment, if he didn't get the votes to show differently. It was important when you look at the statements he made and even his attitude.

At the February 22 School Committee meeting (originally set as the contract vote meeting), the influential CPAC and Bi-lingual Masterpac took Spillane to task for deficiencies in the city's bi-lingual education programs which they documented in a one-half inch report. They pressed for changing the contract vote date to allow time for an evaluation of Spillane's speech (on March 2). At the meeting, O'Bryant supported the request and proposed that the vote be moved to March 8. McKeigue stood firm and called for the vote on March 3.

One week before the March 3 vote, contention again developed over the date of the contract vote. This time, however, Spillane and O'Bryant became the focus for a resolution. In a series of eleventh hour meetings held March 1 and 2 prompted by CFB, a possible delay of the vote was negotiated. For Spillane the delay meant the possibility of getting a unanimous vote; for O'Bryant the delay was a significant "symbolic concession" he could bring to his constituency who had been pressing him to oppose Spillane's re-appointment. McKeigue conceded to a resolution and moved the contract vote to March 8.

For some observers, though, the delay was only a continuation of a consistent strategy employed by O'Bryant that started before the February 8 meeting. "Bud had two votes on his contract," recalled one school official. "Then [a news reporter] really started pushing what O'Bryant was saying about violence is a racial code word…Well, that just about locked in the third vote without even trying; it drew the racial lines which made it impossible for the individual to cross over…So, he got the third vote when really the individual could have gone either way."

Spillane recalled, "O'Bryant made contact with the third (white) school committee member…he was trying to hold up the process and get concessions, trying to make a deal with the third member…but it was a dead-end…they [O'Bryant and McGuire] thought now it was their time since things were being turned around from the white Irish Catholic patronage that raped the system."

Spillane's speech came off without a hitch. Before an audience of 200 people, he detailed his stance on desegregation, staffing, school violence, bi-lingual and secondary education. He addressed McGuire's requirement to be "clear as a bell" about his pre-integration position. "I couldn't believe it," commented one minority parent leader, "It was like a different individual in there."[28] King added, "I think there's no question that in some measure he has come to understand that the black and [Hispanic] community is a power to be reckoned with…He knows he can't go around making those off-the-wall statements and get away with it."[29]

The speech was an embryonic rapprochement: complete support evaded Spillane. One parent leader said her organization would not keep Spillane under siege but promised to be "vigilant" and "monitor his activity...If he lives up to what he says, we will be the first to support him."[30] Others, like James Kelly of the South Boston Information Center, an anti-busing advocate, were less than hopeful and criticized Spillane's appeasement strategy.

Spillane admitted the speech was

> A tricky tactic...You're always going to say something that will trigger a response and sometimes that goes against you...but I tried to be very careful. It was a tough speech for me because I couldn't change the substance of what I was saying but at the same time I had to adjust my style.

Spillane had to find the key phrases to counter the code words which stirred the racial controversy over his contract. He admitted to a given strategy. He talked to people about what to say and not to say. These comments became the "pieces of the puzzle;" then it was written in pieces and re-written from the perspective of delivery. When the speech was ready, it was reviewed again by key individuals for its treatment of sensitive areas. Remarkably, the speech was prepared in a week, sandwiched between a 3-day conference out of town.

Spillane did not get a unanimous vote; instead, the School Committee voted 4–1, with McGuire voting against the re-appointment. McGuire noted the vote entailed "precipitous haste" and explained that with a four-year term available, a new search should be conducted to find a candidate with more urban experience.[31] She added,

> I voted no because I didn't think he was the best person we could get for the job at all...You need a superintendent, a leader of the school system who's not just a good manager...but (one) who's a leader...[and one who] had implicitly in his or her experience a complete understanding and ease of operation and relationship with the constituency the school system serves.[32]

The Study

Preface

This study profiles the first year of Boston Public School Superintendent Robert R. Spillane from August, 1981, to July, 1982. It identifies and discusses the strategies Spillane used to manage the Boston Public Schools in the first year, the reasons for these strategies, and the results.

The study contends that the first year is a critical period for addressing the complexity of urban school system management. It is guided by two questions: What does a new urban superintendent do in the first year? Why does he or she do it?

It is retrospective study and relies on semi-structured interviews and document analysis as the principal sources of data collection. I interviewed Spillane and members of his staff during the first year to gain a sense of recent history and understand the socio-political structure of the school system. But the bulk of the field investigation was completed from September to December, 1982. During this time, I conducted sixty-three interviews with the central office staff, field staff and school system organizations, prominent business and civic organizations, municipal offices, influential parent groups and community organizations, college and university administrations and the Federal Court.

I write a descriptive account that integrates the data into an interpretative framework and explains what Spillane did in the first year and why he did it. The account offers a perspective about the first year. For Spillane's first year, the account presents the network of relationships between Spillane and the school organization, emphasizes the influence of an historical context on management, presents Spillane's perception and response to individuals and constituencies in the diverse and varied Boston environment, focuses the importance of power dynamics, explores interest group relationships and consensus-building, gives attention to how remedial law influences policy making and implementation and creates barriers for effective management, presents curriculum development as a political and management process as well as a pedagogical exercise, identifies the subtleties of building public support and confidence in urban schools and comments on some specific features and roles required by the job.

My analysis suggests the first year for Spillane was a time for building a media protocol and promoting an image, establishing credibility within the school organization and the community, promoting a network of support, setting a professional agenda that resolves some issues and creates a momentum for solving other issues, building a leadership consensus, and focusing administrative authority.

I don't offer a prescription for new urban superintendents. Indeed, issues, individuals and circumstances are different across management environments. For example, Spillane was an outsider; he did not come with "baggage" as one school observer noted. He could create commitments rather than be encumbered by them. Spillane was given an eleven-month contract rather than a long-term contract. This gave him a short-term mentality and put him in a "consultant mode," as one university official put it. Spillane reflected,

> *If I had come in here the first day and they knew I had four years, it may have been a little different...But, I knew I only had 11 months. So, I said the hell with this; let's have some fun and get the God damn place straightened out and whether I make it or not, I won't care. I'll leave Boston a heck of a lot better place than I found it.*

It created, as some observers noted, an "impulsiveness and quickness" to get things done. One noted, "Boston is a small town, things don't change that rapidly. That made Spillane an anomaly...change was quick and caught everyone off guard...before you knew it, he had control."

What I try to do, however, is provide an understanding of urban school system management and, in particular, an understanding of an important stage of tenure, the first year. There are also several reasons why I chose to conduct this study. First, it tells an important story. To many school observers nationally, the Boston Public Schools was one of the most troubled in the nation. I wanted to learn what a new superintendent could do given this reputation. Second, I was also drawn to the study by my own experiences. Formerly a superintendent in a medium-size school district, I wanted to learn more about urban school system management. In fact, when I pursued this interest, I found only a few examples that recorded specific accounts of what an urban superintendent does from the perspective of a field investigation. Finally, I was curious about "first moves": How does a new urban superintendent decide what to do first? What are the first moves and why? I wanted to expose the variables (and their relationships) that affect the first year. I probed the data to find these variables—i.e., power dynamics, citizen status, school resources, client motivation and history. Ultimately (and hopefully), the study will prompt research concerning these variables and their relationships in the first year.

The First Year

Decisions in the first year can be like "quick drying cement...that locks in a new administration even before it gets moving."[1] In addition, demands in the first year create a complex, pressure-packed environment. Warner expresses this view when he notes,

> The [school] superintendent comes into a pre-existing socio-cultural complex with all its local values, beliefs, prejudices, and ground rules of what "to do" and "not to do." He must adjust to, and become part of, a social system he did not help create. He is compelled by the pressures around him to organize his thoughts and activities in accordance with the demands made upon him...[2]

And the risks are high in the first year. The volley of crises that confront a new urban superintendent means he or she must react quickly to many expectations. Until formal systems are defined, "ad-hocracy tends to triumph...[and] mistakes and miscues proliferate."[3] The following attack by one employee toward Spillane illustrates this point: "When he came here he spent all is time charming the business, academic, and political community...but he spent little time winning over, or even attempting to win over, the constituents of this system. That's made it easy for them to turn on him."[4]

First years for urban superintendents are common. Cuban notes that from 1970 to 1973, twenty new superintendents were hired in the 25 largest cities.[5] Still further, the July 2, 1981 issue of the *Wall Street Journal* reports that from 1978 to 1981, sixteen new superintendents were hired in the 28 largest cities.[6]

The study provides an understanding of this period in an urban superintendent's tenure. It is important for two reasons. First, the study tells an important story about urban school system management. Knowing what happened in Boston and what Spillane did (and did not do) adds substantially to the literature. Cuban notes,

> *Few studies in the last decade have been undertaken to investigate how urban schoolmen functioned in the job and to explain why they functioned the way they did. Our lack of in-depth knowledge about the urban school chief...[is] truly awesome...we can document with a fair degree of precision that urban school administrators are, and have been, beset by conflicting cross-currents of pressure; however, few studies have found any pattern of responses to these forces.*[7]

Second, the study provides important information for both practitioners and researchers. Practitioners can see the results of certain strategies. In addition, the study can provoke insights for superintendents who are expecting a tenure in a large, urban school system. And, the study can explore the variables that affect the first year. It can prompt research concerning these variables and their relationships that affect this stage of urban school system management.

Methodology

I interviewed Spillane on a regular basis. These interviews were like debriefing sessions.[8] They focused on specific issues and events so I could get his reflections and impressions about what he did and why he did it. I interviewed a cross-section of individuals to gather another perspective about the first year.[9] Informants were drawn from the central office administration and field staff as well as school system organizations like the Boston Teachers Union, prominent business and civic organizations and the Mayor's office, the Boston City Council, influential parent groups and community-based organizations, college and university administrations, and the Federal court. These interviews exposed the roles and relationships that emerged in the first year and the process of re-shaping the school system in the first year. They exposed the changing character of school desegregation, the political infrastructure that existed in Boston, the lingering effects of history (patronage), and the political dynamics of special interest groups. Since I had a work space in and became part of the central office environment, I held many informal, "on the spot" interviews. These interviews enriched the formal interview data.[10]

I also reviewed important documents like policy statements, documents of public record, memoranda, and speeches. And I chronicled and analyzed Spillane's first year from a two foot pile of news clippings saved by the Public Information Officer.[11]

I analyzed the data as I collected it. I re-wrote my interviews and noted the patterns and trends as I found them.[12] I kept a record of this analysis. More importantly, I used this analysis to revise my interview guide to include new questions, delete some and revise others. Essentially, I relied on an inductive process that encouraged both processing and re-processing raw field data. This helped me to verify the data and reduce bias. In addition, I kept a field journal. This journal recorded my preliminary interpretations of the data.[13]

When I examined the interview data, I found five issues were important in Spillane's first year. In fact, when I tallied the responses to the question (in my interview guide): What were the major issues in the first year?, the results confirmed this focus.

I let the data tell me the story of the first year. When I compared what informants said about an issue, an outline for discussing the issue emerged. I then used the patterns and trends I found and interpretations I made to confirm and expand the outline. I wrote each chapter from these outlines.

The Study

I decided that the best way to tell the story was to treat each issue separately and expose its particular focus and color even though they were essentially occurring at the same time. Each provided a separate dimension that could only be understood by prerogatives being imposed on them in the first year.

As I wrote each chapter, I began to see how they were related. In fact, I was struck by the number of themes that ran through each chapter. These themes are the findings from the case study.

One theme is control. The case study reveals that it is important to establish control over two critical areas: delegated functions and legislated responsibilities. Delegated functions include such things as staff supervision, resource allocation and program implementation. It was important for Spillane to bring these functions closer to his office so that he could set the direction of the school system and monitor its progress. Legislated functions include the delivery of instructional services. Spillane found the responsibility for the delivery of these services stretched over many layers of the complex school bureaucracy. He turned to an accountability program and evaluation protocols to focus his control and build public support.

Another theme is influence. To be sure, some influence emanates from the position; however, the study illustrates that, at times, influence emerges by "flexing one's muscles." He was direct about this view when he said, "You can't be a doormat for every individual and organization." To exercise influence, Spillane relied on exposing educational perspectives and management prerogatives to issues that were politically motivated. In doing so, he defended his "turf" and focused his administration and position in the environment.

A third theme is complexity. The study notes there is an inextricable link between management strategies and environmental expectations. Spillane's reorganization and accountability initiates were directly related to public support issues. Reorganization had to encompass legitimate appointments to benefit a black constituency and accountability had to reflect the interests of the taxpayers who saw the schools as "notoriously mismanaged."

This complexity prompts a fourth theme: choices and tradeoffs. Spillane's first year was a constant series of choices and tradeoffs. His push to reduce spending in order to stay within a mandated budget weakened his efforts to build morale and promote a consensus. Likewise, his confrontation with the Boston Teachers Union to win back management rights (seniority) prompted a coalition that threatened his administration.

Finally, power is a theme.[14] In this study, I refer to power as the capacity to exercise control. It identifies the relationship between power and priorities the first year. In particular, Spillane was vulnerable in the first year; he lacked power. His first moves were designed to build power. He chose priorities that could appeal to certain constituencies who could give him power. He relied on priorities that could weaken the position of his adversaries. In particular, he relied on a high visibility and media focus to expose the political motivations of others and debate issues in public. In short, Spillane's power was intended to do two things: focus his control over others and neutralize the power of others.

Chapter 9
Crossroads: Overview of Confrontations in the First Year

The confrontations were an intriguing part of Spillane's first year. They were theater for Spillane, a way he could step into the public arena and play to a larger audience. An analysis of the public statements Spillane made during each confrontation reveals he wanted to be visible in the first year; he wanted to project a high media profile in order to focus his position in the environment. One news reporter, writing about the first year, noted,

> *Those running battles, detractors suggest, demonstrate that Spillane loathes sharing power, craves public attention and likes to fight. Critics have coined nicknames for him: the Iron Fist in the Velvet Glove, the Macho Superintendent, and the Hit Man [from New York]. Spillane supporters see him as a decisive, candid and a strong manager who gets things done. So what, they argue, if he is a bit impatient and impulsive.*[1]

Spillane admitted, in an interview (with the reporter), "I'll take the rap for being impatient," but then qualified his response by saying: "I don't create conflict. The nature of this job is conflict because it is so complex…I say what's on my mind. I think it's important for people to know where I stand."[2]

The number and complexity of crises facing Spillane in the first year prompted one school official to suggest this was an advantage to him. "Boston was perceived to be at the bottom," he commented. "This gave him license to be more unconventional not only in the positions he took but also in style. Thus, rather than opting for, as one editorial advised, "a blueprint for the schools...a compelling vision for the future,"[3] Spillane adopted a "point-by-point plan" more in the character of a "Patton than a Montgomery." Spillane knew his tough demeanor and confrontational style would appeal to a larger audience (public) and used the confrontations to play to this audience. He reflected,

> *It's important that you don't wait for the crisis. That means you've got to take on as many fronts as you can handle...it was a way to sell myself...if people had confidence in me then they would have confidence in what I do.*

At the time of the teacher layoffs and the threat of a strike, Spillane was also confronting the curriculum incident. He was embroiled in a controversy with two critical areas of urban school system management: the teachers' union and the bureaucracy. The curriculum incident gained momentum and became inflamed at the same time Spillane began his attacks on busing and the Federal Court. This continued up to his re-appointment, and it was at that point that these crises came together in one climatic confrontation.

The confrontations focus the drama of the first year. To be sure, commented a number of school observers, Spillane could have avoided them. He could have negotiated with O'Bryant in the curriculum incident and even over his contract vote (prior to CFB intervention). But the confrontations, the analysis suggests, were a significant part of the job in the first year. Indeed, they illustrate a character about the first year.

The confrontations illustrate the significance of constituency support.[4] The contract vote shows how various constituencies supported Spillane, and even O'Bryant. Likewise, the layoffs and the curriculum incident reveal constituency support was a significant factor in deflecting criticism. One type of support stands out: the media. The media strongly supported Spillane's layoff strategy as well as his efforts to produce a curriculum document. In both cases, this support helped to get School Committee members behind Spillane's initiatives.

The confrontations illustrate the imperatives of the first year. One imperative is establishing administrative authority.[5] In particular, the curriculum incident was more than a matter of producing a curriculum document; it was a matter of exercising the right to delegate responsibilities and even hire and fire staff in order to accomplish certain priorities. Likewise, the threat of a teachers' strike focused on administrative authority. It opened the door to begin a campaign to wrestle management rights away from the BTU. Another imperative is dealing with politics. The layoffs make this point. Spillane's fight for the layoffs was an important effort to control spending when the School Committee was still intrigued with avoiding them for political reasons (image). And, the contract vote surfaces political dealings in an effort to thwart Spillane's bid for re-appointment. Interestingly, both cases reveal the School Committee voting preferences remained unknown until the time of the vote. A third imperative is dealing with a racial environment. Indeed, each confrontation involved a racial issue that was difficult to resolve. In fact, even his supporters pointed out (to me) that Spillane "misunderstood the impact of minorities." One was more direct: "He moved too quickly and didn't consider race carefully enough and stepped on the court's toes. Miller and her honchos were court appointments, and he didn't familiarize himself with that." As a result, Spillane, at times, backtracked on issues and made deals after succumbing to pressures to negotiate a resolution. This waffling tarnished his image.

The confrontations illustrate the complexity of the first year. One school observer commented,

> If you don't address these issues in the first year, then they might trample you later, like curriculum. That had to be done as well as fiscal stuff...It seems the bigger the issue, the faster you have to act but not like what the (Boston) Globe suggested...to have a five year plan...You can't say I'll handle the teacher union next year, the curriculum next year...all these issues intermesh and really you don't have the time.

The confrontations reveal this complexity in three ways. First, they reveal that crises do not come in neat time packages but rather linger throughout the first year. Indeed, the confrontations overlapped and gave Spillane's first year a unique character. Second, they reveal an urgency. Spillane had to face the curriculum incident and the layoffs in order to build credibility with certain constituencies. Had he backed off from both confrontations, the discussion suggests, he would have lost important momentum for his administration. Third, the confrontations reveal how issues intermesh. For example, the layoffs were an economic issue that were also meant to build public support for the schools. Likewise, the curriculum incident reflects Spillane's efforts to establish control as well as focus curriculum development initiatives.

Finally, the confrontations show that Spillane was abiding by the rules of the Boston environment; the forum for debate was the public as well as the discussion table, and dialogue was open (media) as well as closed (negotiations). One editorial put it this way:

> *Boston has seen a fair amount of confrontation over issues...in recent years; and the fact is that confrontation politics will almost surely remain as a necessary part of the local scene.*[6]

Spillane adapted well to this environment; indeed, his temperament was suited to this style of politics. He could easily adjust to spar with the BTU, parent groups, minority interests and even school committee members. In fact, on one occasion, he remarked, that the confrontations were important in the first year: "If you don't do it in the first year, stand your ground, then you'll never do it...you can't be a doormat for every person and organization." But, as even he admitted later, he could have done it differently and "could have been a little more thoughtful."

The process of school governance in Boston was "confrontation politics" which engendered a lack of commitment for building a bi-partisan coalition of human resources. Spillane had a choice: either conform to the history or try to change it. He chose to conform to it. One former Boston Superintendent, in an article he wrote about his experiences, noted,

> *There is a rationality involved, but it is essentially a political one—compromising, not optimizing, enhancing a power base, not carrying out a program...the [process] has been thoroughly politicized...[the skills are] political: coalition-building, consent-inducing, image-projecting, compromise, and waffling.*[7]

Spillane noted in interviews that the School Committee was "like five different corporations; they never talked to one another and told each other how they would vote." Each member was a political advocate; they pressed issues and points of view that reflected political self-aggrandizement. Keeping a level of autonomy, a distance, and even encouraging a mystery about voting habits were important strategies.

Chapter 10
Conclusions

This chapter concludes the study. It stands back from the study and looks more carefully at Spillane's first year so it can be helpful to practitioners and researchers. There is also an attempt to reveal the complexity involved in the management of not only large but also smaller public school organizations; to emphasize the myriad of prerogatives that influence decisions; and, to convey the importance of preparing school leaders who can successfully navigate this terrain.

First Year Strategies[1]

One strategy Spillane used in the first year was building a power base. Spillane's power base included individuals who could exert influence over school issues as well as generate support for his administration. He relied on the Mayor, business community and taxpayers to provide him with important support for his initiatives. One school official wondered, even though Spillane proposed budget reductions that seemed fair, if Spillane had "the political clout to pull it off." Spillane's power base gave him this political clout. They supported his recommendations for teacher layoffs and even lobbied the School Committee to support his position in response to the threat of a teachers' strike. The power base provided leverage for Spillane. They endorsed his efforts at accountability and, moreover, his plans to implement a school-based management project. The power base provided Spillane with influence; he was able to emerge as a key actor in the community along with other key actors and accrue important dividends. The School Committee, seeing the influential support Spillane developed, deferred to the initiatives that had the backing of the Mayor and business community. He noted, "This is the year when I build leverage and a political base and influence. This is what I'm concentrating on...I've got to be careful not to get lost in a long-range thinking." Finally, the power base served as a window on the environment and exposed important clues about the political infrastructure of the city. They were, in a sense, a communication network—a way for Spillane to understand important signals from the environment (even the bureaucracy) and make choices based on relevant information.

Another strategy Spillane relied on in the first year was establishing credibility; it was important to demonstrate his ability to manage and control the Boston Public Schools. In doing so, he earned the confidence of a majority of the School Committee, the Mayor and the business community. His financial credibility gave him leverage in the budget allocation process. Where others sought supplemental funds for the school system, even the School Committee, it was Spillane whom the Mayor deferred to for requests. In addition, Spillane's racial credibility with some black administrators as a result of his minority appointments gave him leverage with black organizations that pushed for affirmative action in the teaching and administrative ranks.

Credibility provided Spillane with important support. Spillane's management credibility promoted support, even loyalty, within the bureaucracy. Spillane's willingness, even risk-taking, to rely on existing personnel in his first year deflated bureaucratic apathy and encouraged a new tone in school affairs. In addition, management credibility earned him the support of the power brokers who backed his reorganization efforts.

Credibility gave Spillane a base for redefining issues. Spillane's management credibility reinforced his accusations that the Federal court intruded into the management of the school system. He could accuse the court of management intrusions because he had shown he could manage the Boston Public Schools. He had, in a sense, earned the right to speak as a manager.

Busing is a good example. Busing was projected as a racial issue since it was considered a remedy for a segregated school system. Spillane had a choice: he could accept the definition or he could try to manage it. He opted to manage it, or, at least, give it a new significance. He did this by redefining busing as an educational issue, by stressing in interviews and speeches "what was at the end of the bus ride." Indeed, he relied on statistics to show that the quality of education was far below average. Furthermore, it was evident from school enrollments that the schools were more segregated than when the court order was first implemented. These were existing weaknesses Spillane relied on to redefine the issue so he could "kick the issue off the dime" and win support for this initiative even though he was on the job less than two months. This suggests he moved quickly in his first year to shore up certain segments in the community to support issues he knew he needed to face. Indeed, the selection of certain blacks to key positions helped to balance the criticisms of racism. The issues intermesh: certain management decisions (staffing) helped him to win the support of blacks in order to confront the Judge. Likewise, financial initiatives garnished support from the business community and the Mayor who saw the Judge as an impediment to their own goals. And, efforts to revitalize the curriculum and establish academic credentials for the school system buoyed his efforts to redefine racial issues in terms of quality education.

In addition, Spillane's professional credibility as an educator, as a result of his curriculum efforts, allowed him to broaden the meaning of public support to include non-clients as well as clients. The media played an important role. While no evidence was available about how it happened, Spillane's memo to the School Committee found its way to the media. This stirred notions that he was grandstanding or playing to the press since he realized he would be criticized along racial lines. (Indeed, it was reported, that Spillane used a strategy like this in a former position to thwart a School Committee's plan to appoint their own person as Spillane's new assistant.)[2]

Spillane relied on the media to present his arguments against the OCC curriculum effort and defend his moves to re-write it. This strategy allowed him to define the issue in terms of curriculum and professional goals rather than confront O'Bryant's claim of exercising poor judgement in the management of the school department. Indeed, even O'Bryant used the media successfully to press his claim, arouse parent support and stir racial commentary.

As it turned out, Spillane did get favorable support for his position from the media. One editorial, using selections of his memo, excused his "arbitrariness" and "impulsiveness" in deference to getting a "meaningful curriculum."[3]

The incident reflects how the imperatives of the first year influenced Spillane. It was important, even critical, for Spillane to publish some document in order to establish his credibility. He did not have another two years to write a curriculum involving the teachers and central office staff. Thus, he faced a choice: either accept the OCC effort or re-write it "from the top" without the customary leadership effort that includes input from others. One school commentator noted,

> I'm sure he thought the hell with a collaborative effort...We need a curriculum. Bea Miller and her little group were working away cheerfully...teacher-to-teacher gradually depositing a linking approach and preoccupied with multi-cultural objectives...then Bud comes in and says this is curriculum. . .

Finally, Spillane relied on promoting an image as a strategy in the first year; it was important to encourage a perception about his ability to manage the schools and to address issues and problems. His tough demeanor against the threat of a teachers' strike, many observers noted, prevented the strike; they (teachers) believed he would fire them if they went on strike. In addition, Spillane's tough stand on accountability gave him leverage with the taxpayers and the business community. They saw accountability as a way to rid the school system of mismanagement. Image-making built a media protocol. Spillane's high visibility in the media encouraged it to turn to him for school positions and views. As a result, he was able to respond to criticisms such as a lack of racial sensitivity and management diplomacy. Image-making allowed Spillane to focus his role in school affairs. It provided him with an opportunity to balance school politics with educational perspectives. The public discussions about busing and desegregation are two examples where an educational perspective was needed to balance existing views. Finally, image-making promoted an identity for Spillane. It dispelled questions like "who is the new superintendent?" that surface in the first year. This was important.

Otherwise, a mystery surrounds the first year and promotes misinterpretations about what is happening and who is making it happen.

Critical Skills

Three critical skills surface from the study: using the media, setting an agenda, and building a network.

Using the Media

Perhaps sensing the importance of the media, Spillane encouraged an "open-door" policy with them. He advertised this policy at meetings he had with editors, publishers and writers during his first two months. In addition, he established a one-person public information office to keep communications open with the media. Since my research desk was located just outside this office, I became very familiar with the activity of the office and its inhabitant, Ian Forman. He was usually on the phone with the media, giving a reaction to an article or explaining a position. More importantly, though, Forman, taking cues from Spillane, used this base of operations to move an issue in a certain direction. A number of in-house quotes found their way into print.

Spillane relied on the media, particularly the press, for a number of things. He relied on the media to expose the subtleties of issues he faced in the first year. "Busing is a failure" opened up a stream of comments that highlighted views hidden in the environment. It focused the discussion around whether desegregation should serve as a way for equal opportunity or quality education. Spillane relied on the media to build a psychological edge on the issues he addressed and the crises he confronted. Spillane's commitment to the teacher layoffs stirred constituencies to push school committee members to support his fiscal initiatives. Likewise, Spillane's attacks on the Federal court's intrusions into the management of the school system prompted others to support his position for management control. Finally, Spillane relied on the media to let people know where he stood on an issue; the media provided a forum for debating issues in public. He used the media to debate the merits of seniority as well as focus his claim that the Federal court order caused a re-segregation of the public schools. More importantly, this forum also surfaced the motivations of others. Spillane's battles with John O'Bryant were a way to surface the staffing designs O'Bryant had on the school system. One school official noted,

> *The media helped him to have others respond publicly. Like, the media goes out and wants to speak to others but they may not want to respond, but then they end up doing so.*

The media was a natural outlet for Spillane's ability to debate issues in public. Still, certain caution existed. The media is an imprecise instrument, and using it is like doing surgery with dull instruments. There was never complete control over what got in the press or how it was written. Forman found, "other things dulled the attempt to use the media such as events that you don't plan on and headlines…It's like punting (in football), you don't know where the ball is going to bounce…that's why it's so important to keep an open dialogue. If you're good at it, then use it; if not, then don't. He was good at it and especially able to make statements that were quotable…he was quick with a sharp quote."

In exercising this caution, Spillane relied on three things. He did not argue with the press who he noted "buys ink by the barrel." Rather, it was important to keep a positive relationship with them and rely on them to argue with his critics and convey messages to his supporters. Second, he established a policy so that crises had a specific spokesperson. In fact, it was a general policy that in times of crises there was only one spokesperson. In most cases, Forman usually conveyed sentiments and rebuttals on how certain crises (and issues) were handled by the press. At other times, attorneys and deputy superintendents were charged with specific "spokesperson rights." Third, the study reveals, Spillane relied more on "talk" rather than press releases to convey his positions. He noted,

> *You don't put out press releases to respond to critical issues…they're good for giving information about a program, giving statistics and maybe even whetting the appetite of a reporter. But many releases never make it…hot items do, the sexy items do…So you've got to talk about them…no press release can or will replace that.*

Spillane issued few press releases and conducted only three press conferences in his first year. It was a choice: talk replaced formal dialogue and gave Spillane an advantage. One BTU official noted,

> *He would tell me privately when he was unhappy with something we did...and suggest he might have to use the press...he's doing that because now it's mostly his position that takes precedence.*

Using the media in the first year was important to promote positions. In addition, it was important in order to deflect misinterpretations and move issues in a certain direction; to gather important momentum.

Setting an Agenda

Spillane's agenda was predicted on certain priorities. When I listed the priorities of each constituency in the city, the priorities that found their way to Spillane's agenda reflected the interests of the power brokers. Indeed, Spillane's agenda evolved, and even changed, according to the concerns of these powerful actors in the city. What emerges, then, and what school observers made clear to me is that Spillane's agenda for the first year was not based on a reflection of what he thought should be done but rather what the key actors in the community felt should be done.[4]

Spillane's agenda reflected a time dimension. Certain issues were dealt with on a short-run basis; others were relegated to a long-run basis. Short-run issues included fiscal management control (reorganization). These were important to do immediately. More importantly, though, these short-run issues needed to reflect target dates. Each month, Spillane showed evidence, some visible sign, that the agenda was being implemented. For example, the layoffs in September were evidence that Spillane would "live within a $210 million budget." Likewise, his comments that "spending would be under control by December" were signals to the business community and taxpayers.

Long-run issues played a different role on the agenda. "You've got to have certain things launched in the first year," commented one school official. For Spillane, accountability and curriculum initiatives were long-run issues that served as a way of gathering momentum. The impact of these initiatives would be felt in later years. One school official criticized Spillane for not addressing the teacher absenteeism problem. He noted,

> *They (teacher absences) last year were the largest in recent years...People were saying "The hell with this; if I'm going to be laid-off, I'll take my time now." That feeling ran all across the city. Plus, those that stayed kept saying "This is crazy. This guy is taking time off while I'm here." He (Spillane) didn't really address that...there was no enforcement.*

Spillane did not go after the teacher absenteeism problem; rather he set in motion an accountability program that could get at the issue. It reflected a choice of agenda items and a choice of which constituent expectation he addressed. Likewise, the teacher contract, which curtailed his management authority, was also a long-run issue. He used the first year to build a momentum for a time he could confront the contract; for the time when it became a short-run issue. One school observer noted,

> *Spillane used the first year to put a stamp on the way things were going...not necessarily to see the conclusion of everything but just to put a direction on the issues so they headed for a suitable conclusion...The first year really served as a way of gathering momentum.*

Short-run issues put Spillane's agenda in a reactive mode. These issues had a short life expectancy; they were meant to be removed from the agenda by the end of the first year. Long-run issues put Spillane in a proactive mode. They were meant to set the stage for addressing other issues at another time. Indeed, an analysis of the data reveals there is a relationship between accountability and school-based management initiatives in the first year and teacher negotiations planned for the second year; a relationship between curriculum initiatives in the first year and the improvement of instruction and student performance planned for later years.

The agenda focused staff energy. Spillane made reconciling the school department's books with the city auditor's records an important concern. When, in fact, he could claim they were in agreement, an unusual and neglected accomplishment in previous years, he took to the media to herald the event. In a sense, the agenda was important because it set the framework for prioritizing items on his staff's agenda.

Even long-run issues on the agenda focused staff energy. For example, each of the crises, or confrontations, Spillane dealt with in the first year were tied to long-run issues. The threat of a teachers' strike laid the foundation for addressing seniority and the curriculum incident focused on establishing management authority.

Building a Network

The Boston School Superintendent holds a seat on the Public Facilities Commission that plans new schools. Six years ago, the Superintendent never got to sit on the Commission. Up to two years ago, there was a parliamentary move so that the seat would not be available to the Superintendent…But Spillane now sits on that Commission.

Spillane established a network with key actors in the city. They helped him to set an agenda, build credibility, and promote an image. Indeed, this network illustrates the importance of establishing positive relationships with certain groups. These relationships reflect two characteristics: exchange and stability.

Spillane's network relied heavily on exchanges each participant could provide. Both the Mayor and the business community needed a school system that was fiscally responsible. Both suffered at the hands of a runaway budget. Spillane was in a position to relieve this anxiety and respond to their needs. In turn, the Mayor and the business community were in a position to provide Spillane with important support. There was, then, an exchange of influence of position.

The same kind of exchange characterized his relationship with the School Committee. The School Committee was dependent on Spillane to improve their image and Spillane needed their support for his re-appointment. Spillane reflected,

Looking back over the first year, what really seemed important, even crucial, was two choices: work through the School Committee or work through the public which means the media. But the two are tied togeth-

er. The trick is to get along with the School Committee through the media. They see the kind of image I build benefits them as well...When I take a case to the public, it can also benefit them. I look good, they look good.

Spillane's relationship with the School Committee highlights the sensitivity of exchange. At least three school committee members, it was pointed out to me, voted for his re-appointment based on "I look good, they look good." They identified with Spillane's financial and management initiatives so that they won important constituent support. One school observer commented, "They were always getting the back of the Mayor's hand. Now they were beginning to see some of the front. It was an important change in attitude and image."

There was, then, an important link between Spillane's network of power brokers and the School Committee. Some school observers I spoke with sensed it was Spillane's way of establishing control over the School Committee because they were dependent on him to improve their image. But Spillane's failure to get approval for two mid-year layoff recommendations and a black school committee member's hesitancy to support his re-appointment reveal something else. They reveal that while Spillane built his own network, other networks existed and deflected, at times, his attempt to control the School Committee. Other networks included the Federal court and minority parents, parent groups and certain school committee members, the black leadership in the school and minority parents and the unions. Depending on the issue, anyone of these networks could join hands with other networks to form a coalition that could, and did, actively confront Spillane and his network.

The existence of these networks makes stability elusive. Even though Spillane's network supported his re-appointment, they urged, even pushed, him to negotiate a peace settlement with minority interests who did not support his re-appointment. Indeed, the coalition that surfaced around minority interests—the black leadership and the CPAC—gave Spillane's network cause for concern. In order to maintain stability with his network, Spillane had to defer to their motivations.

Stability is elusive for another reason. Individual networks formed coalitions around issues; they saw exchange among themselves as important as exchange within the network. The contract vote makes this point. For example, even Spillane's network approached the leaders of minority interests to prompt an accord. The BTU, displeased with Spillane's attitude toward them, supported minority parents when they voiced concern over budget and program cuts. It was not unusual to find, at times, white school committee members joining with black school committee members to defeat layoff and appointment recommendations made by Spillane.

Rather than forming a coalition on the basis of a common goal, sometimes coalitions were formed on the basis of self-interest. The BTU, for example, sought to deflect Spillane's offensive toward them, while minority parents sought resources. White school committee members were concerned about morale, black school committee members were concerned about affirmative action.

These two characteristics—exchange and stability—that emerge from the data suggest it is important to map the environment in the first year. This requires two things. First, it requires identifying the sets of relationships that exist and clarifying the perceptions of each relationship. All these perceptions make up the urban school system environment. Second, it requires separating those relationships that need special attention from those with a more general problem. The second point is crucial; it provides the foundation for building a network (and setting an agenda). Specifically, Spillane felt the power brokers needed special attention; he built a network with them and their concerns became agenda priorities. However, Spillane viewed minority interests a general problem; even affirmative action, took a back seat, at times, to management control.

Afterthoughts

Spillane comes out a winner in this study, but there are critics who would disagree. Indeed, a critical look at the first year reveals it entailed costs for both Spillane and the school system. There was a price paid for the choices Spillane made and the approach he took to manage the Boston Public Schools in his first year. This can be seen in a number of ways.

On two occasions in the study I asked: did Spillane choose (his constituency) correctly? On one hand, Spillane deferred to the interests of the power brokers; in fact, his media focus was intended in part to play to this audience. On the other hand, Spillane did not court the support of parents, particularly minority parents. This constituency looked to him to build a cooperative leadership for the clients of the school system; that is, an effort that could build an accord among the ethnic, racial and linguistic minorities in the school system. He did not make this effort, and in doing so, he failed to address one of the most important issues facing the Boston Public Schools. He created a rivalry between the school administration and parents that encouraged opposing missions and interest. It may be costly since this strategy created barriers for effective communication with an important constituency.

The tone that Spillane established when dealing with parents may echo later in his tenure. Toward the end of his first year, the Federal court reorganized parent groups and streamlined them into one collaborative organization. He entered his second year facing a more unified parent constituency rather than the diversity of parent groups he found in his first year. This gave parents a new significance and legitimacy when, essentially, he could have accomplished the same thing through a more conscious leadership effort. One court official noted, "I don't think that was the way he should have worked with parents. What you're doing is managing people so you have to work with them. It's a difficult thing to do because of the cross-currents and forces playing on a superintendent such as social, political and economic things, and even power dynamics. But what seems important is to get constituencies together and bring them into a team and guide them to your way of thinking."

In the long run, Spillane may also have affected an important criterion on which he will be judged: getting parents to be willing to send their children to the Boston Public Schools. School observers commented, that unless and until parents feel they have a share in the decision making process and a voice in the education of their children, it is unlikely that school enrollments will increase.

Even though Spillane was acknowledged for his management skill, school observers questioned his tact and diplomacy. His "top-down" approach to curriculum and accountability may be costly in later years. The successful implementation of the curriculum objectives (in order to raise student performance) depends a great deal on whether teachers believe in the new city-wide objectives. Without participating in their development, it is unlikely they will have a "feeling of ownership," to use Spillane's pedagogy. Spillane's high-handed approach may well spark a counter-bureaucracy and threaten his efforts to revitalize the curriculum. Indeed, he needs this professional cadre to develop a solid educational program and, in turn, win back confidence in the schools and increase enrollments.

Likewise, Spillane's heavy-handed approach with the teachers' union created problems. To be sure, he needed to regain management rights and to assert that the superintendent is a full partner in the plans and programs of the school system. However, as the study notes, this approach may be costly since it created a rivalry with the teachers' union and costs may include a strike at the next negotiation session.

"The public likes you to be tough, but at the same they want you to have class," commented one school official. This suggests there is a need for balance between substance and style, action and purpose. Spillane's first year included examples of how he alienated people and overlooked important issues. His attacks on the Federal court and especially Judge Garrity, the black school committee members and parent leaders suggest an inability to interact with a wide range of personalities. Likewise, his comments about busing reflect an insensitivity to racial issues and his media campaign against the curriculum writing effort suggest a "bull-like" quality when dealing with the staff. This approach will leave scars, as the study notes, and cost Spillane important support for initiatives later in his tenure. Especially with the staff, this approach may foster a defensive attitude where missed assignments will be cloaked with comments like, "it wasn't my responsibility."

Spillane left indicators at the end of his first year that suggest a rising tide of apprehension and opposition rather than unity. Early policy decisions and program initiatives neglected the input and collaboration of important individuals who, in turn, can sabotage implementation. Spillane enters his second year with deferred time bombs that can explode at any time. These are the costs that can be traced to how the first year was played out.

The point that emerges is that the choice of and relationships between strategies and skills was an entangling dilemma for Spillane in his first year. One miscue may well have made the first year his last year. In fact, he told me after he won his four-year contract: "You almost wrote about my last year, not my first."

Coming close to this circumstance suggests it is important to look at the first year in a different way, indeed a detached view. Spillane had a number of things in his favor that gave him an advantage in the first year.

Spillane was the right guy at the right time. The Boston Public Schools were plagued by mismanagement and a poor image. In addition, the schools lacked a sense of direction. He noted,

> *I had the overall impression that it was chaotic. There was no system-wide information. Record keeping for students was at best sloppy...But even on the other side, there was a sense of absolute frustration. I mean "who's the next superintendent?" I was the fourth one in [fourteen months]. They really wanted some stability in the system, some leadership from the central office so that they could do their jobs.*[1]

These conditions suited Spillane's management orientation. He relied on his knowledge and experience to install basic management techniques and a new organizational structure. Even Spillane admitted: "I was confident that I was going to be successful. No question in my mind. I had to be because I wasn't inventing a new wheel. I mean systems have been running well and managed for decades. We're just getting into the nineteenth century." As a result, his moves to promote stability and improve the public image of the schools fell on fertile soil.

In another respect, Spillane was also the right guy in the right place. His natural bent toward politics and self-confidence matched the political climate of the city. He adjusted well to the environment that focused on confrontation politics. While this had benefits for the schools, it also had benefits for Spillane. Stated bluntly, the media exposure boosted his ego, promoted his self-esteem and raised his confidence. He was the right guy in the right place because the environment allowed decisions to emerge from politicized discussions; indeed, Spillane preferred that kind of "working climate". He managed the school system in the first year because he was permitted to practice "the art of confrontation politics, the art of coalition and mobilization politics and the uncompromising art of compromise."[2] His first year was not his last because of this marriage of style and environment.

Spillane was also able to meld his ability of knowledge to what existed. The school system, and particularly the school department, lacked a focus and a spokesperson. Spillane's inclination toward visibility and a commanding presence in school affairs filled that void. One school commentator noted,

> The best way to describe him is that he was a public relations person. He was always in the newspapers, on the radio, T.V., even in the national press...He saw that as his job and everything else as someone else's job.

There was a need to be met. A school official remarked, "It was bravado for the troops. He took a stand which meant a lot...people were looking for someone to say yes or no. The interim superintendents couldn't give any answers and didn't have any visibility so we used to talk to the press and go on television but there wasn't any focus. He got the focus for the schools."

There was also a sense of urgency and priority to solve the school's problems when Spillane took over the job. This was an advantage to him. He did not have to be prodded to make a "quick study"; it was congruent with his approach to management. One school official close to Spillane recalled,

> *He usually didn't have a lot of patience with a problem but just liked to get them done...just action-oriented. Like there are things that used to be treated as policy so we used to discuss them for hours. Now they just get done.*

This urgency provided a suitable accommodation. Indeed, the data reveal, he was more decision- and action-orientated than reflective and contemplative, even impulsive and impatient. He could get away with a top-down management style rather than involving others in specific initiatives—i.e., curriculum development.

Spillane also had room in which to move in the first year; that is, he had latitude in the environment to make choices that were in agreement with his prescriptions for solving the problems of the Boston Public Schools. He could choose the power brokers as his support and ally over parent groups. Two reasons come to mind. First, parent groups were in disarray and lacked a united front to severely threaten his initiatives. (Even the contract vote suggests that Spillane was assured at least a 3–2 vote in favor of his re-appointment.) Second, the power brokers were on the margin of school politics but wanted a role in improving the schools. He found them receptive to his overtures and supportive of his initiatives.

In another respect, the clients were not the focus of Spillane's initiatives in the first year. He was able to hold their priorities to a later time and concentrate on financial and management control. He could leave program improvement and student achievement to later years and even cut programs and budgets without seriously handicapping his credibility. The environment allowed him to make choices that benefited him. Spillane recollected,

> *I just knew what was wrong and went about trying to solve those major management issues like personnel, budget, management information, curriculum, special education, bi-lingual education...What are the most*

important? Solve the bi-lingual issues and problems. Hell, no. Get your budget under control so at least you know how much you have…and that you're not going to run out.

Finally, Spillane was the benefactor of a changing climate in school affairs. If he came a few years earlier, he would not have found a school committee committed to fiscal responsibility. Even parent groups were willing to defer priorities for management and financial initiatives and business groups were willing to help by providing technical assistance to "straighten out the mess." And, after nearly a decade of Federal court intervention, he found a climate that encouraged the withdrawal of the court from the Boston School Desegregation Case.

What Spillane did and why he did it was contingent upon the circumstances he found. The discussion implies there was a fit between Spillane and the environment, skills and needs, knowledge and problems. Without this fit, his success would have been short-lived.

If the environment was less prone to confrontation politics, he would have stirred anxieties and lost influence; if the school system had a focus, a presence, his visibility would have been challenged and his image-making strategies (debating issues in public, taking public positions) would have backfired; if an urgency did not exist, his quick remedies to problems would have been less palatable and poorly received for want of debate; and, if a different climate existed, he would have found his fiscal control initiatives buttonholed, a greater resistance by patronage recipients and an explosion over how he saw the court. Had he come even two or three years before, Spillane's first year may well have been his last. But, "ifs" don't make first years. This study argues that an accommodation between the environment and management skill, leadership and style make first years.

Notes

Boston: The City and Its Actors

1. The terms were used in various newspaper articles and in speeches given by Superintendent Spillane.
2. Robert R. Spillane, "Building Effective Schools," NAESP/NASSP Seminar for Officers of Large City Administrator Associations, December 3, 1981.
3. Fred C. Doolittle, George S. Masnick, Phillip L. Clay and Gregory A. Jackson, *Future Boston Patterns and Perspectives* (Cambridge, MA: The Joint Center for Urban Studies of MIT and Harvard University, 1982), p. 1.
4. Ibid., p. 1.
5. *The Boston Globe*, November 4, 1981, p. 15.

Chapter 1 — Teacher Layoffs

1. *The Boston Globe*, August 7, 1981, p. 1.
2. *The Boston Globe*, August 14, 1981, p. 3.
3. Ibid.
4. Ibid.
5. *Boston Herald American*, August 14, 1981, p. 1.
6. *The Boston Globe*, August 17, 1981, p. 9.
7. *The Boston Globe*, August 19, 1981, p. 1.
8. Ibid., p. 28.
9. *Boston Herald American*, August 19, 1981, p. 1.
10. *The Boston Globe*, August 17, 1981, p. 9.
11. Robert R. Spillane, speech to Principals, Headmasters, and Other Key Personnel, August 26, 1981.

12. *Boston Herald American*, August 29, 1981, p. 1.

13. Ibid.

14. Ibid., p. A4.

15. Ibid.

16. Ibid.

17. Robert A. Dentler and Marvin B. Scott, *Schools On Trial An Inside Account of the Boston Desegregation Case* (Cambridge, MA: Abt Books, 1981), p. 192.

18. Ibid.

19. *The Boston Globe*, September 18, 1981, p. 15.

20. *The Boston Globe*, September 7, 1981, p. 1.

21. *Boston Herald American*, September 6, 1981, p. 1.

22. *Boston Herald American*, August 29, 1981, p. 1.

23. *The Boston Globe*, September 7, 1981, p. 26.

24. *Boston Herald American*, September 7, 1981, p. A4.

25. *Boston Ledger*, Week of September 6–13, 1982, p. 10.

26. *Boston Herald American*, September 20, 1981, p. 4.

27. *Boston Ledger*, Week of September 6–13, 1982, p. 10.

28. *Boston Herald American*, May 20, 1982, p. 17.

29. *Boston Herald American*, June 2, 1982, p. 17.

Chapter 2 — A Nightmare

1. *The Boston Globe*, December 1, 1981, p. 17.

2. *The Boston Globe*, July 31, 1981, p. 1.

3. Ibid., p. 22.

4. *The Boston Globe*, August 15, 1981, p. 15.

5. Robert Wood, "Beyond Implementation: The Case of the Boston Public Schools," Unpublished Manuscript, n.d., pp. 8–9. After this case study was completed, I learned this article was subsequently published—see Robert Wood, "Out of the Trenches Professionals at Bay: Managing Boston's Public Schools," *Journal of Policy Analysis and Management* 1, No. 4 (1982), pp. 454–468.

6. See Robert A. Dentler and Marvin B. Scott, *Schools On Trial An Inside Account of the Boston Desegregation Case* (Cambridge, MA:

Abt Books, 1981), p. 21.
7. Wood, "Beyond Implementation...", p. 6.
8. Ibid., p. 15.
9. *The Boston Globe*, August 26, 1981, p. 16.
10. *The Boston Globe*, December 16, 1981, p. 34.
11. *The Boston Globe*, September 23, 1981, p. 14.
12. *The Boston Globe*, August 15, 1981, p. 15.

Chapter 3 — The Chess Board
1. These are staff members at the time Spillane became superintendent. By the end of Spillane's first year, the *total school staff* (central office and field staff) was reduced by 1801 positions or 20%. Teachers, who represented 57% of the total school staff in FY 81, were cut by 835 (net). The central office staff was reduced by 317 (net) or 30% and the field staff (including teachers) was reduced by 1484 or 18%. Source: Boston Municipal Research Bureau, Special Report, May 14, 1982. No. 82-5.
2. Spillane memorandum, October 14, 1981, p. 1.
3. Ibid., p. 4.
4. *The Boston Globe*, September 15, 1981, p. 22.
5. *The Boston Globe*, July 21, 1982, p. 14.

Chapter 4 — The Incident
1. Robert R. Spillane, "How To Bring Order Out of Chaos: The Boston Experience," speech given at the National School Boards Association Annual Convention, April 17, 1982.
2. Wood, in an interview, described Miller as "terribly well qualified and an intelligent person." But, he added, "whether or not she appropriately organized her office, or whether she is a manager, is probably open to question." *The Boston Globe*, June 22, 1982, p. 12.
3. *The Boston Globe*, June 22, 1982, p. 12.
4. Ibid.
5. Ibid.
6. *Boston Herald American*, November 29, 1981, p. 62.

7.   *Boston Herald American*, November 26, 1981, p. 16.
8.   Ibid.
9.   Also reported by *Boston Herald American*, November 29, 1981, p. 62.
10. *Boston Herald American*, December 10, 1982, p. 10.

Chapter 5 — Blue Books and Red Books

1.   *The Boston Globe*, June 22, 1982, p. 1.
2.   Ibid.
3.   Ibid.
4.   Ibid., p. 12.
5.   *The Boston Globe*, March 20, 1982, p. 11.
6.   *The Boston Globe*, June 22, 1982, p. 12.
7.   Joseph Viteritti, et al., *Transition Report to the Superintendent Boston Public Schools*, September 14, 1981, p. 6.
8.   Robert R. Spillane, "Presentation to the Massachusetts Conference on Children, Youth and Families," November 15, 1981.
9.   *The Boston Globe*, August 23, 1981, p. 43.
10. *The Boston Globe*, June 21, 1982, p. 6. School Department figures varied between 3.2 and 4.6.
11. In many interviews, respondents suggested "the perception of effectiveness and responsiveness counted more, in the short run, than substantive performance." See Victor A. Thompson, *Modern Organizations* (New York: Knopf, 1961), pp. 138–151; and Francis E. Rourke, *Bureaucracy, Politics, and Public Policy*, 2nd ed. (Boston, MA: Little, Brown, 1976), pp. 100–102.
12. "Curriculum and Testing in the Boston Public Schools: A Policy Proposal," January 12, 1982, p. 7.
13. Ibid., p. 8.
14. Ibid., p. 9.
15. Robert R. Spillane, "How to Bring Order Out of Chaos: The Boston Experience," speech given at the National School Boards Association Annual Convention, April 7, 1982.
16. *The Boston Globe*, August 27, 1982, p. 44.

17. "Curriculum and Testing...," p. 7.

18. Ibid., p. 5.

19. Spillane, "How to Bring..."

20. *The Nashua Telegraph*, November 15, 1981, p. 20. Both the BTU and the BASAS joined the chorus. BASAS attributed the violence in the schools to the reduction of assistant principals who enforce school rules and student discipline.

21. Spillane, "How to Bring..."

22. Robert R. Spillane, "Rebuilding the Boston Public School System: The Educational Dimension of the City's Renaissance," speech given to the Phi Delta Kappa Society at Harvard University, September 24, 1981.

23. Ibid.

24. Spillane, "How to Bring..."

25. Ibid.

26. Robert R. Spillane, "Building Effective Schools," NAESP/NASSP Seminar for Officers of Large City Administrator Associations, December 3, 1981.

27. *The Boston Globe*, September 6, 1981, p. 45.

28. The discussion relies on the "Interim Status Report: School Based Management Project," Boston Public Schools, November 1, 1982.

29. *The Boston Globe*, May 23, 1982, p. A4.

30. Ibid., pp. A1, A4.

Chapter 6—A Shadow in My Mirror

1. Robert A. Dentler and Marvin B. Scott, *Schools On Trial An Inside Account of the Boston Desegregation Case* (Cambridge, MA: Abt Books, 1981), p. 3.

2. Dentler and Scott, *Schools on Trial*, p. 10.

3. Ibid., p. 22.

4. Ibid., p. 15.

5. Ibid., p. 31.

6. Ibid., p. 41.

7. Ibid.

8. Ibid., p. 35.
9. *The Boston Globe*, June 24, 1982, p. 31.
10. Robert Wood, "Beyond Implementation: The Case of the Boston Public Schools," Unpublished Manuscript, n.d., p. 13.
11. Dentler and Scott, *Schools on Trial*, p. 190.
12. Ibid., p. 203.
13. Ibid., p. 85.
14. Wood, "Beyond Implementation...", pp. 12–13.
15. *Allston—Brighton Citizen Item*, September 9, 1982, p. 12.
16. *The Boston Globe*, April 22, 1982, p. 41.
17. *Boston Herald American*, April 30, 1982, p. 21.
18. Wood, "Beyond Implementation...", p. 14.
19. *Boston Herald American*, September 28, 1981, p. 3.
20. Ibid.
21. *The Boston Globe*, May 19, 1982, p. 12.

Chapter 7—Public Support

1. *The Boston Globe*, July 28, 1981, p. 2.
2. Robert R. Spillane, speech to Principals, Headmasters, and Other Key Personnel, August 26, 1981.
3. *The Boston Globe*, September 26, 1981, p. 31.
4. Ibid.
5. *The Boston Globe*, March 7, 1982, p. 26.
6. Robert A. Dentler and Marvin B. Scott, *Schools On Trial An Inside Account of the Boston Desegregation Case* (Cambridge, MA: Abt Books, 1981), p. 35.
7. Robert Wood, "Beyond Implementation: The Case of the Boston Public Schools," Unpublished Manuscript, n.d., p. 17.
8. *The Boston Globe*, September 26, 1981, p. 13.
9. *The Boston Globe*, August 15, 1982, p. 70.
10. *Boston Ledger*, Week of September 13–20, 1982, p. 11.

Chapter 8—The Contract Fight

1. Jean Sullivan McKeigue, State of the Schools Message (Inaugural

Address as President of the Boston School Committee), January 11, 1982.

2. *The Boston Globe*, January 25, 1982, p. 40.
3. *The Boston Globe*, February 3, 1982, p. 18. The comments are a summary of the responses given by O'Bryant and McGuire.
4. Ibid.
5. *The Boston Globe*, February 9, 1982, p. 22.
6. *The Boston Globe*, February 14, 1982, p. 36.
7. *Boston Herald American*, February 9, 1982, p. 14.
8. *The Boston Globe*, February 9, 1982, p. 22.
9. *The Boston Globe*, February 4, 1982, p. 36.
10. *The Boston Globe*, February 9, 1982, p. 22.
11. *The Boston Globe*, February 14, 1982, p. 36.
12. *The Boston Globe*, February 9, 1982, p. 1.
13. *Boston Herald American*, February 11, 1982, p. 21.
14. Ibid.
15. *The Boston Globe*, February 8, 1982, p. 18.
16. Ibid.
17. Ibid.
18. *The Boston Globe*, February 10, 1982, p. 41.
19. *The Boston Globe*, March 7, 1982, p. 26.
20. Ibid.
21. Ibid.
22. *The Boston Globe*, March 2, 1982, p. 18.
23. *Boston Herald American*, February 17, 1982, p. 14.
24. *The Boston Globe*, February 17, 1982, p. 1.
25. Ibid.
26. *Christian Science Monitor*, December 24, 1981, p. 84.
27. *The Boston Globe*, March 2, 1982, p. 18.
28. *The Boston Globe*, March 7, 1982, p. 21.
29. Ibid., p. 27.
30. *Boston Herald American*, March 2, 1982, p. 3.
31. *The Boston Globe*, March 7, 1982, p. 27.
32. *The Boston Tab*, March 17, 1982, p. 1.

Preface

1. Donald H. Haider, "Presidential Transitions: Critical, If Not Decisive," *Public Administration Review* 4, No. 2 (March/April 1981), p. 207.

2. Lloyd Warner, *Democracy In Jonesville* (New York: Harper, 1949) quoted in William L. Boyd, "The Public, The Professionals, and Educational Policy Making: Who Governs?" *Teachers College Record* 77, No. 4 (May 1976), p. 539. See also John Merrow, Richard Foster and Nolan Estes, *The Urban School Superintendent of the Future* (Durant, OK: Southwestern Foundation, 1974); and Donald J. McCarty and Charles E. Ramsey, *The School Managers* (Westport, CT: Greenwood Publishing Corp., 1971).

3. Haider, "Presidential Transitions...," p. 209. For an insightful look at the varied and diverse expectations that confront an urban superintendent, see Marilyn Gittell, *Participants and Participation* (New York: Praeger, 1967); Laurence Iannaccone, ed., *Public Participation in Local School Districts* (Lexington, MA: Lexington Books, 1978); and Robert Salisbury, "Schools and Politics in the Big City," *Harvard Educational Review* 27, No. 3 (Summer 1967), pp. 408–424.

4. *Boston Herald American*, February 14, 1982, p. 3.

5. Larry Cuban, *Urban School Chiefs Under Fire* (Chicago: University of Chicago Press, 1976), pp. 172–173. See also Merrow, Foster and Estes, *The Urban School Superintendent of the Future*, esp. chs. 1, 5.

6. Douglass Sease, "School Superintendent, Once Pillar of Society, Now is Often a Target," *Wall Street Journal* (June 2, 1982), p. 19.

7. Cuban, *Urban School Chiefs Under Fire*, p. 111.

8. See especially Henry Mintzberg, *The Nature of Managerial Work* (New York: Harper and Row, 1973), pp. 150–153. Mintzberg points out the importance of this type of interview in order to get at important information that often goes undocumented. He notes that "some [information] is documented and can be made easily available. Much of it, however, exists only in the manager's natural memory and can be disseminated only by word of mouth" (p. 150).

9.   I conducted sixty-three interviews from September to December, 1982. I developed interview guides to conduct these interviews. I gathered divergent perspectives concerning the strategies Spillane used in the first year, why he used them and what happened. The use of multi-perspective cross-checking helped for the purpose of validity and reduction of bias. In order to provide some assurances for the accuracy of the data, I asked at least two individuals all substantive questions.

Because of the sensitive nature of the data presented in the case study, I do not identify interview data, nor date it. My raw field data was collected on the basis of confidentiality and the use of anonymous attribution. Needless to say, I take full responsibility for the interpretation and analysis of the data. Individuals interested in pursuing the data presented here can contact the author.

10. The "spot," as I came to call it, was located at an unused secretary's desk just outside the Public Information Office and in the line of traffic to the Superintendent's office. Individuals stopped by to find out what I was doing and generally the conversation led to their reflection and impression of the first year. However, an important dividend was the opportunity to talk frequently with the Public Information Officer. In the hub of activity, he gave willingly of his time so I could sharpen my interpretations and check my hunches. These informal talks helped to expose the color and drama of the first year.

11. The "clips" were very helpful. I took more than 400 pages of notes. I catalogued these notes by issues and events and cross-filed them by dates. The effort was important for a number of reasons. First, the clips provided the detail for building a chronology of the first year. Second, the clips identified individuals I should interview; in fact, they were the basis for a respondent's file. Third, the clips offered insights to the first year. For example, the use of the media became evident and vividly portrayed the importance of this strategy in the first year. Finally, the clips provided a cross-check to the interview data.

12. See R. Gordon, *Interviewing: Strategies Technologies and Tactics,*

3rd ed. (Homewood, IL: Dorsey Press, 1980); and Gilbert Sax, *Foundations of Educational Research* (Englewood Cliffs, NJ: Prentice-Hall, 1979).

13. See especially Jerome Murphy, *Getting the Facts: A Fieldwork Guide for Evaluators and Policy Analysts* (Santa Monica, CA: Goodyear, 1980), p. 120.

14. See John P. Kotter, *Power in Management* (New York: AMACOM, 1979), esp. chs. 2, 3.

Chapter 9—Crossroads: Overview of Confrontations

1. *The Boston Globe*, August 15, 1982, p. 67.
2. Ibid.
3. *The Boston Globe*, July 7, 1982, p. 14.
4. The analysis suggests a "conflict" environment was a necessary part of Spillane's first year. See John Merrow, Richard Foster and Nolan Estes, *The Urban School Superintendent of the Future* (Durant, OK: Southwestern Foundation, 1974). They advise that unless the tolerance for conflict increases, "urban schools will not be manageable in our times" (p. 96); see also Wes Apker, "Building Power Relationships," *School Administrator* 39, No. 8 (September 1982), p. 15.

5. Spillane faced a dilemma most urban superintendents face; that is, the definition given to the role of each of the participants in the school governance process. See Paul C. Schmidt and F. Voss, "School Boards and Superintendents: Modernizing the Model," *Teachers College Record* 77, No. 4 (May 1976). They note the first task for a new superintendent is "to draw an understanding picture of which duties rightfully belong to the board and which rightfully belong to [the superintendent]. It is the superintendent's first duty and major obligation to straighten out thinking" (p. 520); see also Harmon L. Zeigler, "Creating Responsive Schools," *The Urban Review* 6, No. 4 (1973), pp. 38–44; Harmon L. Zeigler and M.K. Jennings, *Governing American Schools* (North Scituate, MA: Duxbury Press, 1974); and Frederick M. Wirt, "Political Turbulence and Administrative Authority in the Schools," in Louis

H. Masotti and Robert L. Lineberry, eds., *The New Urban Politics* (Cambridge, MA: Ballinger, 1976 b), pp. 61–89.

6. *The Boston Globe*, March 13, 1982, p. 10.

7. Robert Wood, "Beyond Implementation: The Case of the Boston Public Schools," Unpublished Manuscript, n.d., pp. 22–23.

Chapter 10—Conclusions

1. See Robert E. Schiller, "Strategies for New Superintendents," *School Administrator* 39, No. 8 (September, 1982), p. 39.

2. This incident was reported by the *Christian Science Monitor*, December 24, 1981, p. B4.

3. *Boston Herald American*, November 29, 1981, p. 62.

4. A number of authors suggest the conclusion that a small informal elite, whether as members of a school board or "interested parties" wield influence in school districts. See Michael W. Kirst, ed., *The Politics of Education at the Local, State, and Federal Level* (Berkeley, CA: McCutchen, 1970); Guy Benveniste, *The Politics of Expertise* (Berkeley, CA: Boyd and Fraser, 1977); and Frederick M. Wirt and Leslie Christovich, "Are Superintendents Paper Tigers?" *School Administrator* 39, No. 9 (September 1982), pp. 12–13. Wirt and Christovich recently conducted (1981) a national study of superintendents and note, "a clear central finding is that superintendents overwhelmingly report 'more' or 'much more' demands than they had once known in their jobs. Those two responses totaled 60 percent of all answers about business groups and lay opinion…" (p. 12).

Afterthoughts

1. *Boston Ledger*, Week of September 6–13, 1982, p. 17.

2. Wes Apker, "Building Power Relationships," *School Administrator* 39, No. 8 (September 1982), p. 15. See also Laurence Iannoccone, "Superintendents Make a Difference," *School Administrator* 38, No. 8 (September 1981), pp. 16–17; and especially Feilders case study of Robert Alioto, Chief Superintendent of San Francisco Unified School District—John F. Feilders, *Profile The Role of the Chief*

Superintendent of Schools (Belmont, CA: Pitman Learning, Inc., 182).

Bibliography

Aiken, Michael, and Hage, Jerald. "Organizational Interdependence and Intraorganizational Structure." *American Sociological Review* 33 (6), December 1968, pp. 912–930.

Allison, Graham T. *Essence of Decision: Explaining the Cuban Missile Crisis.* Boston, MA: Little, Brown, 1971.

Apker, Wesley. "Building Power Relationships." *School Administrator* 39 (8), September 1982, pp. 14–15.

Argyris, Chris. Overcoming Leadership Effectiveness. New York: John Wiley and Sons, 1976.

———. "Personality and Organizational Theory Revisited." *Administrative Science Quarterly* 18 (2), June 1973, pp. 141–167.

———. *Integrating the Individual and the Organization.* New York: John Wiley and Sons, 1964.

Bacharach, Samuel B. "Organizational and Political Dimensions for Research on School District Governance and Administration." In Samuel B. Bacharach (Ed.), *Organizational Behavior in Schools and School Districts.* New York: Praeger, 1981, pp. 3–43.

Bacharach, Samuel B., and Lawler, Edward J. *Power, Coalitions and Bargaining: The Social Psychology of Organizational Politics.* San Francisco: Jossey-Bass, 1980.

Bailey, Stephen K., et al. *Schoolmen and Politics.* Syracuse, NY: Syracuse University Press, 1962.

Barnard, Chester I. *Functions of the Executive.* Cambridge, MA: Harvard University Press, 1938.

Bennis, Warren. "Leadership: A Beleaguered Species." In David Kolb, Irwin Rabin, and James McIntyre (Eds.), *Organizational Psychology:*

A Book of Readings (3rd ed.). Englewood Cliffs, NJ: Prentice-Hall, 1979, pp. 330–343.

Benveniste, Guy. *The Politics of Expertise*. Berkeley, CA: Boyd and Fraser, 1977.

Boyd, William L. "The Public, The Professionals, and Educational Policy Making: Who Governs?" *Teachers College Record* 12 (4), May 1976, pp. 539–577.

Burger, Anthony E. *Paul Ryland. Superintendent of Schools: An Ethnographic Account*. Unpublished doctoral dissertation, University of Pittsburgh, 1978.

Burlingame, Martin. Superintendent Power Retention. In Samuel B. Bacharach (Ed.), Organizational Behavior In Schools and Scr.ooi Districts. New York: Praeger, 1981, pp. 429–463.

Campbell, Roald F. "The World of the School Superintendent." *New York University Education Quarterly* I (1), Fall 1977, pp. 14–20.

Campbell, Roald, F., Cunningham. L. L., and McPhee, R. P. *The Organization and Control of American Schools* (4th ed.). Columbus, OH: Charles Merrill, 1980.

Carlson, Richard O. *School Superintendents: Career and Performances*. Columbus, OH: Charles Merrill, 1972.

Cistone, Peter J. *Understanding School Boards*. Lexington, MA: Lexington Books, 1975.

Cleveland, Harlan. "A Philosophy for the Public Executive." In Robert T. Golembiewski (Ed.), *Perspective on Public Management Cases and Learning Designs*. Itasca, IL: F. E. Peacock, 1979, pp. 12–33.

Corwin, Ronald. *Education in Crisis*. New York: John Wiley and Sons, 1974.

——. Professional Persons in Public Organizations. *Educational Administration Quarterly* 1 (3), Autumn 1965, pp. 1–22.

Crain, Robert L. *The Politics of School Desegregation*. New York: Aldine, 1968.

Cronin, Joseph. *Control of Urban Schools*. New York: Free Press, 1973.

——. "The School Superintendent in the Crucible of Urban Politics." In Frank W. Lutz (Ed.), *Toward Improved Urban Education*. Worthington, OH: Charles A. Jones, 1970.

Cronin, Joseph, and Hailer, N. *Organizing an Urban School System for Diversity: A Report on the Boston Public School Department.* Cambridge, MA: McBer, 1970.

Cuban, Larry. *Urban School Chiefs Under Fire.* Chicago: University of Chicago Press, 1976.

Deal, Terrence E., and Colotti, Lynn. "Loose Coupling and the School Administrator." Stanford Center for Research and Development in Teaching, Stanford University, 1977.

Dentler, Robert A., and Scott, Harvin B. *Schools on Trial: An Inside Account of the Boston Desegregation Case.* Cambridge, MA: Abt Books, 1981.

Denzin, N. K. *The Research Act: A Theoretical Introduction to Sociological Methods.* Chicago, IL: Aldine, 1970.

Doolittle, Fred C., Masnick, George S., Clay, Phillip L., and Jackson, Gregory A. *Future Boston Patterns and Perspectives.* Cambridge, MA: The Joint Center for Urban Studies of MIT and Harvard University, 1982.

Downs, Anthony. *Inside Bureaucracy.* Boston, MA: Little, Brown, 1967.

Educational Policies Commission. *The Unique Role of the Superintendent of Schools.* Washington, DC: National Educational Association, 1965.

Emory, F. E., and Trist, E. L. "The Causal Texture of Organizational Environments." *Human Relations* 18 (2), 1965, pp. 268–281.

Erickson, Donald A. "Moral Dilemmas of Administrative Powerlessness." *Administrator's Notebook* 20 (8), April 1972, pp. 1–4.

Feilders, John F. *Profile: The Role of the Chief Superintendent of Schools.* Belmont, CA: Pitman Learning, Inc., 1982.

Gates, Philip E., Blanchard, Kenneth H., and Hersey, Paul. "Diagnosing Educational Leadership Problems: A Situational Approach." *Educational Leadership* 33 (5), February 1976, pp. 348–354.

Gittell, Marilyn. *Participants and Participation.* New York: Praeger, 1967.

Gittell, Marilyn, and Hollander, T. E. *Six Urban School Districts.* New York: Praeger, 1968.

Goldhammer, Keith. *The School Board.* New York: Center for Applied Research, 1964, Chapter 1.

Gordon, R. *Interviewing: Strategies, Technologies and Tactics* (3rd ed.). Homewood, IL: Dorsey Press, 1980.

Guthrie, Janes W., and Skene, Paula H. "The Escalation or Pedagogical Politics." *Phi Delta Kappan* 54 (6), February 1973, pp. 386–389.

Hage, J. *Communication and Organizational Control.* New York: John Wiley and Sons, 1974.

——. "An Axiomatic Theory of Organization." *Administrative Science Quarterly* 10 (3), December 1965, pp. 289–320.

Haider, Donald H. "Presidential Transitions: Critical, If Not Decisive." *Public Administration Review* 4 (2), March/April 1981, pp. 207–211.

Hall, Richard H. *Organization's Structure and Processes* (2nd ed.). Englewood Cliffs, NJ: Prentice Hall, 1977.

Hanson, E. Mark. "Organizational Control In Educational Systems: A Case

Study of Governance In the Schools." In Samuel B. Bacharach (Ed.), *Organizational Behavior in Schools and School Districts.* New York: Praeger, 1981, pp. 245–275.

Hentschke, Guilbert C. "Reform In Urban School District Policy Making: Comparing the 'Watchdog' and the 'Thinktank.'" *Educational Administration Quarterly* 16 (2), Spring 1980, pp. 77–99.

Howe II, Harold. "The Care and Feeding of Superintendents." *Saturday Review*, February 17, 1962, p. 52.

Hoy, Wayne K., and Miskel, Cecil G. *Educational Administration Theory, Research, and Practice* (2nd ed.). New York: Random House, 1982.

Hoy, Wayne K., and Williams, Leonard B. "Loyalty to Immediate Superior at Alternate Levels in Public Schools." *Educational Administration Quarterly* 7 (2), Spring 1971, pp. 1–11.

Hoyle, John R. "Urban Education 1999 Alternative Futures." *Education and Urban Society* 13 (3), May 1981, pp. 357–380.

Iannaccone, Laurence. "Superintendents Make a Difference." *School Administrator* 38 (8), September 1981, pp. 16–17.

——. (Ed.). *Public Participation in Local School Districts.* Lexington, MA: Lexington Books, 1978.

Iannaccone, Laurence, and Cistone, Peter J. *The Politics of Education.*

Eugene, OR: ERIC Clearinghouse on Educational Management, 1974.

Ianni, F. A., and Orr, M. "Toward A Rapproaoheaent of Quantitative and Qualitative Methodologies." In T. D. Cook and C. S. Reichardt (Eds.), *Qualitative and Quantitative Methods in Evaluative Research*. Beverly Hills, CA: SAGE, 1979.

Katz, Ralph. "Job Longevity As a Situational Factor in Job Satisfaction." *Administrative Science Quarterly* 23 (2), June 1978, pp. 204–223.

Kaufman, Herbert. "Fear of Bureaucracy: A Raging Pandemic." *Public Administration Review* 4 (1), January/February 1981, pp. 1–9.

Kennedy, M. "Generalizing From Single Case Studies." *Evaluation Quarterly* 3 (4), November 1979, pp. 661–678.

Kerr, Norman D. "The School Board As an Agency of Legislation." *Sociology of Education* 38 (3), Autumn 1964, pp. 34–59.

Kimbrough, Ralph. *Political Power and Educational Decision-Making*. Chicago: Rand McNally, 1964.

Kirp, David I. "Race, Schooling, and Interest Politics: The Oakland Story." *School Review* 78 (4), August 1979, pp. 355–397.

Kirst, Hichael W. (Ed.). *State. School, and Politics*. Lexington, MA: D. C. Heath, 1972.

——. (Ed.), *The Politics of Education at the Local, State, and Federal Level*. Berkeley, CA: McCutcher, 1970, pp. 1–9.

Knezevich, Stephen J. (Ed.). *The American School Superintendent*. Washington, DC: American Association of School Administrators, 1971.

Kotter, John P. *Power in Management*. New York: AMACOM, 1979.

Lawrence, Paul R., and Lorsch, Jay W. *Organization and Environment; Managing Differentiation and Integration*. Boston, MA: Graduate School of Business Administration, Harvard University, 1967.

Levenson, William B. *The Spiral Curriculum: The Urban School in Transition*. New York: Rand McNally, 1968, Chapters 5, 6 and 12.

Levin, Henry (Ed.). *Community Control of Schools*. Washington, DC: Brookings Institute, 1970.

Licata, Joseph W., and Hack, Walter G. "School Administration

Grapevine Structure." *Educational Administration Quarterly* 16 (3), Fall 1960, pp. 82–89.

Lorsch, Jay W., and Morse, J. J. *Organizations and Their Members: A Contingency Approach.* New York: Harper and Row, 1974.

Lyke, Robert F. "Representation and Urban School Boards." In Henry H. Levin (Ed.), *Community Control of Schools.* Washington, DC: Brookings Institute, 1970, pp. 138–168.

McCaffrey, Michael D. "Politics In the Schools: A Case for Partisan Board Elections." *Educational Administration Quarterly* 7 (3), Autumn 1977, pp. 51–83.

McCarty, Donald J., and Ramsey, Charles B. *The School Managers.* Westport, CT: Greenwood Publishing Corp., 1971.

McGivney, Joseph H., and Haught, James M. "The Politics of Education: A View from the Perspective of the Central Office Staff." *Educational Administration Quarterly* 8 (3), Autumn 1972, pp. 18–38.

McGivney, Joseph H., arnd Moynihan, Wm. "School and Community." *Teachers College Record* 74 (2), December 1972, pp. 209–224.

Maeroff, Gene I. "Harried School Leaders See Their Role Waning." *The New York Times.* March 5, 1970, pp. 1; 29.

Manch, Joseph. "The Urban Superintendenoy as Viewed By a Survivor." *Phi Delta Kappa* 58 (4), December 1976, pp. 348–349.

Mann, Dale. *The Politics of Administrative Representation.* Lexington, MA: Lexington Books, 1976.

——. "Public Understanding and Education Decision Making." *Educational Administration Quarterly* 10 (2), Spring 1970, pp. 1–18.

March, James C., and March, James G. "Almost Random Careers: The Wisconsin School Superintendency." *Administrative Science Quarterly* 22 (3), September 1977, pp. 337–409.

March, James G. "American Public School Administration: A Short Analysis." *School Review* 86 (2), February 1978, pp. 217–245.

March James G., and Olsen J. P. *Ambiguity and Choice in Organizations.* Bergen, Norway: Universitetsforlaget, 1976.

Masotti, Louis H., and Lineberry, Robert L. (Eds.). *The New Urban Politics.* Cambridge, MA: Ballinger, 1976.

Marrow, John, Foster, Richard, and Estes, Nolan. *The Urban School Superintendent of the Future*. Durant, OK: Southeastern Foundation, 1970.

Meyer, John W., and Rowan, Brian. "The Structure of Educational Organizations." In Marshall W. Meyer et al. (Eds.), *Environments and Organizations*. San Francisco: Jossey-Bass, 1978, pp. 78–109.

——. "Institutionalized Organizations: Formal Structure as Myth and Ceremony." *American Journal of Sociology* 22 (3), September 1977, pp. 377–409.

Minar, David W. "The Community Basis of Conflict in School System Politics." *American Sociological Review* 31 (6), December 1966, pp. 822–834.

——. "Community Characteristics, Conflict, and Power Structures." In Robort S. Cahill and Stephen P. Heneley (Eds.), *The Politics of Education in the Local Community*. Danville, IL: Interstate Printers and Publishers, 1964.

Mintzberg, Henry. *The Nature of Managerial Work*. New York: Harper and Row, 1973.

Moser, Robert. "The Leadership Patterns of School Superintendents and School Principals." *Administrator's Notebook*, September 1957.

Murphy, J. *Getting the Facts—A Fieldwork Guide for Evaluators and Policy Analysts*. Santa Monica, CA: Goodyear, 1980.

Peterson, Paul E. *School Politics Chicago Style*. Chicago: University of Chicago Press, 1976.

Pitner, N. J. *So Go the Days of Their Lives: A Descriptive Study of the Superintendency*. Eugene: University of Oregon (Oregon School Study Council, Vol. 18, No. 5, January 1979).

Presthus, Robert. *The Organizational Society*. New York: Alfred Knopf, 1962. Chapters 6, 7, and 8.

Raffel, Jeffrey A. "A Review of *The Neighborhood Based Politics of Education* (by H. L. Summerfield)." *Harvard Educational Review* 42 (1), February 1972, pp. 126–139.

Ravitch, Diane, and Goodenow, Ronald K. *Educating an Urban People: The New York City Experience*. New York: Teachers College Press, 1981.

Reddin, William J. *Managerial Effectiveness*. New York: McGraw Hill, 1970.

Robbins, Stephen P. *The Administrative Process: Integrating Theory and Practice*. Englewood Cliffs, NJ: Prentice-Hall, 1976.

Rogers, David. *The Management of Big Cities: Interest Groups and Social Change Strategies*. Beverly Hills, CA: Sage, 1971.

———. *110 Livingston Street*. New York: Random House, 1968.

Rourke, Francis E. *Bureaucracy, Politics, and Public Policy* (2nd Ed.). Boston, MA: Little, Brown, 1976.

Salisbury, Robert. "Schools and Politics in the Big City." *Harvard Educational Review* 37 (3), Summer 1967, pp. 408–424.

Sax, Gilbert. *Foundations of Educational Research*. Englewood Cliffs, NJ: Prentice-Hall, 1979.

Schiller, Robert S. "Strategies for New Superintendents." *School Administrator* 39 (8), September 1982, p. 36.

Schmidt, Paul C. and Voss, F. "Schoolboards and Superintendents: Modernizing the Model." *Teachers College Record* 77 (4), May 1979, pp. 517–526.

Scott, H. J. "The Urban Superintendency on the Brink." *Phi Delta Kappan* 58 (4), December 1976, pp. 347–348.

Scott, W. Richard. *Organizations Rational, Natural, and Open Systems*. Englewood Cliffs, NJ: Prentice-Hall, 1981.

Sease, Douglass. "School Superintendent, Once Pillar of Society, Now Is Often a Target." *Wall Street Journal*, June 2, 1982, pp. 1; 19.

Sergiovanni, Thomas J., and Carver, P. D. *The New School Executive*. New York: Harper and Row, 1980.

Sergiovanni, Thomas J., and Starratt, Robert J. *Emerging Patterns of Supervision: Human Perspectives*. New York: McGraw-Hill, 1979.

Simon, Herbert A. *Administrative Behavior* (2nd ed.). New York: Macmillan, 1957.

Spiegel, Jacob J., Keppel, Francis, McCormick Jr., Edward, and Willie, Charles V. *Report of the Masters in Tallulah Morgan, et al. versus John Kerrigan, et al*. U.S. District Court, Boston, Massachusetts, March 31, 1975.

Spradley, James P. *Participant Observation*. New York: Holt, Rinehart and Winston, 1980.

———. *The Ethnographic Interview*. New York: Holt, Rinehart and Winston, 1979.

Stake, Robert. "The Case Study Method in Social Inquiry." *Educational Researcher* 1 (2), February 1978, pp. 5–7.

Starratt, Robert J. "Contemporary Talk as Leadership: Too Many Kings in the Parade?" *Notre Dame Journal of Education* 4 (11), Spring 1973, pp. 5–14.

Staw, Barry, and Salenolk, C. (Eds.). *New Directions In Organizational Research*. New York: St. Clair Press, 1977.

Steele, Donald J., Working, Russell J., and Biernacki, Gerald J. "Care and Feeding of Interest Groups: Interest Groups As Seen By a City School Superintendent." *Education and Urban Society* 13 (2), February 1981, pp. 257–270.

Sullivan, Neil, V. *Walk, Run or Retreat: The Modern School Administrator*. Bloomington: Indiana University Press, 1971.

Terreberry, Shirley. "Evolution of Organizational Environments." *Administrative Science Quarterly* 12 (4), March 1968, pp. 590–613.

"The School Superintendency: The Impossible Job." *Education U.S.A.*, March 4, 1974, p. 145.

Thompson, James D. *Organizations in Action*. New York: McGraw-Hill, 1967.

Thompson, John T. *Policy-making in American Education*. Englewood Cliffs, NJ: Prentice-Hall, 1976.

Thompson, Victor A. *Modern Organizations*. New York: Alfred A. Knopf, 1961.

Tucker, Harvey J., and Zeigler, Harmon, L. *Professionals Versus the Public: Attitudes, Communication, and Response In School Districts*. New York: Longman, 1980.

Tyack, David B. *The One Best System: A History of American Urban Education*. Cambridge, MA: Harvard University Press, 1974.

Vidich, Arthur J., and Bensman, Joseph. *Small Town in Mass Society*. Princeton, NJ: Princeton University Press, 1968.

Viteritti, Joseph P. "Policy Analysis in the Bureaucracy: An Ad-hoc Approach." Unpublished Manuscript, n.d.

Viteritti, Joseph P., and Carponcy, Daniel G. "Information, Organization and Control: A Study of System Application." *Public Administration Review* 4 (2), March/Aprll 1981, pp. 253–260.

Webb, Eugene J., Campbell, Donald T., Schwartz, Richard D., and Grove, *Janet B. Nonreactlve Measures in the Social Sciences* (2nd ed.). Hopewell, NJ: Houghton Mifflin Company, 1981.

Weeres, Joseph B. "School-Community Conflict in a Large Urban School System." *Administrator's Notebook* 19 (9), May 1971, pp. 1–4.

Weick, Karl E. "Educational Organizations as Loosely Coupled Systems." *Administrative Science Quarterly* 21 (1), March 1976, pp. 1–19.

Weiss, Carol. *Evaluation Research: Methods for Assessing Program Effectiveness.* Englewood Cliffs, NJ: Prentice-Hall, 1972.

Willower, D. J., and Fraser, H. W. "School Superintendents on Their Work." *Administrator's Notebook* 28 (2), January 1980, pp. 1–4.

Wirt, Frederick M. "Education, Politics and Policies." In Herbert Jacobs and Kenneth Vines (Eds.), *Politics in the American States: A Comparative Analysis.* Boston, MA: Little, Brown, 1976a, pp. 284–349.

——. "Political Turbulence and Administrative Authority in the Schools." In Louis H. Masotti and Robert L. Lineberry (Eds.), *The New Urban Politics.* Cambridge, MA: Ballinger, 1976b, pp. 61–89.

Wirt, Frederick M., and Christovich, Leslie. "Are Superintendents Paper Tigers?" *School Administrator* 39 (8), September 1982, pp. 12–13.

Wirt, Frederick M., and Kirst, Michael W. *The Politics of Education: Schools in Conflict.* Berkeley, CA: McCutchen, 1982.

——. *The Political Web of American Schools.* Boston, MA: Little, Brown. 1975.

Wood, Robert. "Professionals at Bay: Managing Boston's Public Schools." *Journal of Policy Analysis and Management* 1 (4), 1982, pp. 454–468.

Zald, Mayer N. "The Power and Functions of Boards of Directors." *American Journal of Sociology* 75 (7), July 1969, pp. 97–111.

Zeigler, Harmon L. "Creating Responsive Schools." *The Urban Review* 6 (4), 1973, pp. 38–44.

Zeigler, Harmon L., and Jennings, M. K. *Governing American Schools.* North Scituate, MA: Duxbury Press, 1974.

Acknowledgments

Before this became a story of "Bud" Spillane's first year as the Boston superintendent, it was my dissertation at Harvard University in 1983. In completing the dissertation, I incurred many debts. My largest is to the many educators at Harvard Graduate School of Education for their guidance and encouragement, especially Greg Jackson, my advisor. From the preparation and design of the field study to the final draft, he was a friend when I was tired, a counsel when I was confused, a critic when I thought I was right and, most of all, a skillful navigator. He successfully guided me through waters and jagged rocks of research protocol and responsibility. I became a better practitioner because of him. I am indebted to Harold "Doc" Howe, former U.S. Commissioner of Education under President Johnson, for his interest and concern for the study. His thoughtful commentary shaped the style and structure of the final draft. It was "Doc" who suggested the study of "Bud" Spillane who was new to Boston. My thanks also go to Jerome Murphy. His critical assessment of my drafts focused the data. From him I came to understand and respect analysis.

As I began to formulate my plans for the study, John Kotter at the Business School offered important advice. He guided me through my first attempts at interviewing and patiently eased my anxiety. Later, Sue Johnson reviewed my interview guides and offered suggestions which paid enormous dividends. Joseph Viteritti saw me through an extensive review of the literature. He encouraged me to pursue the study of the first year and focused my attempts to organize the data.

To my good fortune, Robert R. "Bud" Spillane's first year coincided with my desire to do the study. His cooperation and willingness to open up his administration to prying eyes made this study possible. He gave me time when I needed it and gracefully and humorously eased my uncertainty as I went about Boston. The story emerged because of his honesty and character. I am thankful to many of Spillane's staff for their help, especially his secretary, Mary Caton. She promply and gracefully answered my questions and fulfilled my requests for documents, policies, and so on. Ian Fleming, the Pubic Relation Officer, provided the background information behind the events and always said yes when I asked him for a minute.

In making the transition from a dissertation to an important story in Boston's history, I am grateful to Joni Cullan for her enormous patience and skill. She typed and retyped sections as I edited and re-edited the narrative so it reflected a readable pace and style. She always kept her composure and helped me keep mine. I am thankful for her friendship.

Finally, my family was always supportive. I want to thank my sons Michael and Timothy for their "willingness" to give me the quiet and serenity as I studied and wrote. And, most important, I want to express my gratitude to my wife Catherine for her understanding and encouragement at every moment. She made my dream a reality.

Julius J. D'Agostino is a retired educator living in eastern Connecticut. Over fifty years he served as principal, assistant superintendent and superintendent of schools, and associate professor in Vermont, New Hampshire, and Connecticut.

Made in the USA
Las Vegas, NV
31 January 2021